Pronunciation Tasks

A course for pre-intermediate learners

Martin Hewings

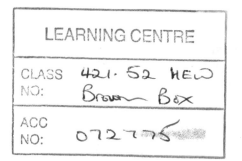

STUDENT'S BOOK

Please check CD
with this book

CAMBRIDGE
UNIVERSITY PRESS

CAMBRIDGE UNIVERSITY PRESS

Cambridge, New York, Melbourne, Madrid, Cape Town, Singapore, São Paulo, Delhi

Cambridge University Press
The Edinburgh Building, Cambridge CB2 8RU, UK

www.cambridge.org
Information on this title: www.cambridge.org/9780521386111

First published 1993
13th printing 2007

Printed in the United Kingdom at the University Press, Cambridge

A catalogue record for this publication is available from the British Library

ISBN   978-0-521-38611-1 Student's Book
ISBN   978-0-521-38610-4 Teacher's Book
ISBN   978-0-521-38453-7 Set of 2 cassettes

Contents

Acknowledgements

I would like to thank:

Jeanne McCarten, Lindsay White and Alison Silver, who so professionally and patiently guided the book through its various stages.

Anne Colwell, Nick Newton and Nicholas Otway for their design work.

The many people who commented on the material and the principles on which it is based. In particular, Michael McCarthy, David Brazil and Richard Cauldwell.

Ann Hewings, Louise Ravelli, Thelma Smith and Peter Hickman who helped make recordings for earlier forms of the material.

The teachers and institutions who worked with the pilot edition, for their many helpful comments.

George Taylor for the illustrations.

Key to phonetic symbols

Vowels

Symbol	Examples
/ɑː/	_arm_ _part_
/æ/	_apple_ _black_
/aɪ/	_eyes_ _drive_
/aʊ/	_out_ _now_
/e/	_end_ _pen_
/eɪ/	_eight_ _day_
/eə/	_air_ _wear_
/ɪ/	_it_ _sit_
/iː/	_eat_ _see_
/ɪə/	_ear_ _near_
/ɒ/	_opposite_ _stop_
/əʊ/	_open_ _phone_
/ɔː/	_always_ _more_
/ɔɪ/	_boy_ _join_
/ʊ/	_would_ _stood_
/uː/	_you_ _choose_
/ʊə/	_sure_ _tourist_
/ɜː/	_early_ _bird_
/ʌ/	_up_ _luck_
/ə/	_ago_ _doctor_

Consonants

Symbol	Examples
/b/	_bed_ _about_
/d/	_do_ _side_
/f/	_fill_ _safe_
/g/	_good_ _big_
/h/	_hat_ _behind_
/j/	_yes_ _you_
/k/	_cat_ _week_
/l/	_lose_ _allow_
/m/	_me_ _lamp_
/n/	_no_ _any_
/p/	_put_ _stop_
/r/	_run_ _around_
/s/	_soon_ _us_
/t/	_talk_ _last_
/v/	_very_ _live_
/w/	_win_ _swim_
/z/	_zoo_ _loves_
/ʃ/	_ship_ _push_
/ʒ/	_measure_ _usual_
/ŋ/	_sing_ _hoping_
/tʃ/	_cheap_ _catch_
/θ/	_thin_ _bath_
/ð/	_then_ _other_
/dʒ/	_June_ _age_

To the student

Who is the book for?

Pronunciation Tasks is for pre-intermediate level students who want to improve their English pronunciation. Many of the tasks will also be useful for higher level students.

It has been written for students working in class with a teacher, although many of the tasks are suitable for students working on their own with a cassette recorder.

How is the book organised?

The book is divided into an Introduction and eight parts. Each part focuses on a particular aspect of English pronunciation, and is divided into eight or nine units.

It is not necessary to work from Unit 1 to Unit 66. Choose units or parts that will help with the pronunciation problems you have.

The cassettes

The cassettes contain all the recordings necessary for the listening and repetition activities in the book. The symbol ⌷ shows that there is a recording for a task on the cassette. The symbol ◄◄ ⌷ means you should rewind the cassette and repeat the recording for the previous task.

Introduction

Unit 1   Asking about pronunciation

Here are some ways of asking how to pronounce words correctly.

Asking about the pronunciation of written words

1   Listen to these conversations.

2   Work in pairs. Ask about the pronunciation of these words. (If you need to check the pronunciations of the words listen to the recording.)

medicine   commercial   chocolate   information   vegetables

Asking if your pronunciation is correct

3   Listen to these conversations.

4 Work in pairs. Use the phrases in the conversations to ask about the pronunciation of these places in Britain. (If you need to check the pronunciations of the words listen to the recording.)

Leicester	Edinburgh	Portsmouth	Norwich	Stratford
Brighton	Carlisle	Worcester		

Asking which pronunciation is correct

5 Listen to these conversations.

6 Are there any words which you are not sure how to pronounce? Ask your teacher about them in the same way.

Part 1   Vowels

Unit 2   The short vowels /æ/, /ɪ/ and /e/

1 Repeat these words and notice the vowel sound /æ/ in each.

> back   hat   map   plan   match

2 Underline the vowels pronounced /æ/ in this conversation.

A: Where were you standing?
B: Outside my flat.
A: Where was the man?
B: He ran out of the bank.
A: Was he carrying anything?
B: A black bag.
A: Thank you, madam.

3 Listen and check your answers. ⊙━

4 Listen again. Repeat the conversation a line at a time. Then work in pairs and say the conversation together.

5 Follow the same steps for these words and conversations. ⊙━

a The sound /ɪ/

> pick   still   if   with   swim

A: This one?
B: A bit big.
A: Let's give her this one, then.
B: Still too big.
A: Will this fit?
B: Yes, I think so. She's quite thin.

b The sound /e/

> press   tell   red   best   help

A: And can you get some eggs?
B: How many?
A: Ten, please.
B: Anything else?
A: Some bread. Do you need any money?
B: No, I'll pay by cheque.

6 Repeat the words in the box.

> a camera   a television   a handbag   a credit card   a stamp
> a swimming costume   a tennis racket   a hat   a sweater
> a fishing rod   some cash   a chess set   some matches   a map
> a tent   your address book   a blanket   some string

7 Work in pairs. Discuss with your partner the *three* most useful things to have when ...

1 ... you are lost in a city.
2 ... you are on holiday.
3 ... your car breaks down.
4 ... you are lost in a forest.

Choose words from the box in **6**.

8 Report your answers to the rest of the class.

Unit 3 The short vowels /ɒ/, /ʊ/ and /ʌ/

1 Match the words in each group that contain the same vowel sound. One is done for you.

watch • • good	just • • push	blood • • book
looks • • stopped	got • • lunch	not • • long
shut • • stuck	pull • • cough	cook • • cut

2 Repeat the words and check your answers. ⊙⇁

3 Now complete these conversations using the pairs of matching words. ⊙⇁
One is done for you.

1 A: What time is it?
   B: Sorry, my *watch*............ has *stopped.*.........

2 A: Aren't you well?
   B: No, I've .... a ....

3 A: What time's the bus?
   B: .... now.

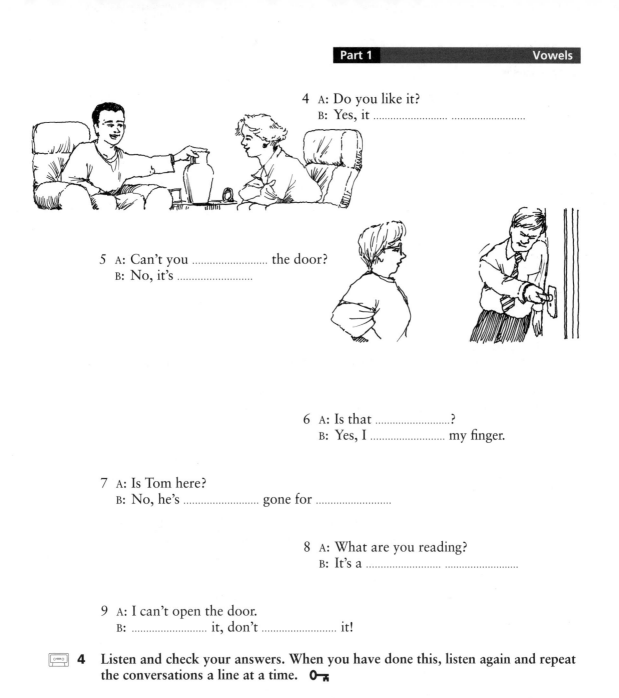

4 A: Do you like it?
   B: Yes, it ....

5 A: Can't you .... the door?
   B: No, it's ....

6 A: Is that .... ?
   B: Yes, I .... my finger.

7 A: Is Tom here?
   B: No, he's .... gone for ....

8 A: What are you reading?
   B: It's a ....

9 A: I can't open the door.
   B: .... it, don't .... it!

4 Listen and check your answers. When you have done this, listen again and repeat the conversations a line at a time. 🔑

5 Work in pairs and say the conversations together.

6 Work in pairs. Think of two things that these adjectives can describe. Some examples for the first are given. 🔑

   1 common   *a common problem* .... , *a common name* ....
   2 good   .... , ...
   3 comfortable .... , ...
   4 horrible   .... , ...
   5 funny   .... , ...

7 Report your answers to the rest of the class.

Unit 4 /ɪ/ & /e/ and /æ/ & /ʌ/

Focus on /ɪ/ and /e/

1 Repeat the words in box A, then the words in box B.

A   B

bill	tin		bell	ten
fill	will		fell	well
lift	spill		left	spell
lit	till		let	tell

2 Work in pairs. Say a word from one of the boxes. Your partner will tell you if it comes from A or B.

3 Listen to these sentences. Do they include words from box A or box B? The first one is done for you.

1 A....   2 ....   3 ....   4 ....   5 ....   6 ....   7 ....   8 ....

Focus on /æ/ and /ʌ/

4 The words in these phrases contain the sounds /æ/ or /ʌ/. (Ignore the words 'a' and 'an'.) They have the following patterns:

An angry customer. = /æ/ + /ʌ/   Come back! = /ʌ/ + /æ/
A lovely summer. = /ʌ/ + /ʌ/   A happy man. = /æ/ + /æ/

Listen to the phrases and write them in this table.

/æ/ + /ʌ/	/ʌ/ + /æ/	/ʌ/ + /ʌ/	/æ/ + /æ/

5 Listen again. Repeat the phrases and check your answers.

6   Use some of the phrases to complete these conversations. 🔑

7   Work in pairs and say the conversations together.

Unit 5   The long vowels /iː/, /ɜː/, /ɑː/, /ɔː/ and /uː/

1   Find four words in the box below that contain the same vowel sound as in:

1 cl<u>ea</u>n   /iː/   ....
2 b<u>ir</u>d   /ɜː/   ....
3 c<u>ar</u>   /ɑː/   ....
4 f<u>our</u>   /ɔː/   ....
5 f<u>oo</u>d   /uː/   ....

and write them in the spaces.

improve	heart	prefer	law	visa	piece	laugh
early	banana	water	me	fruit	June	free
Thursday	word	abroad	half	bought	blue	

2   Repeat the words and check your answers. 🔑

3 Choose words from the boxes on the right and write them in the spaces. The word you choose should have the same (underlined) vowel sound as the vowel (circled) in the line. One is done for you.

1 A: Have you seen............... my n(ie)ce?
  B: Is she the g(ir)l in the skirt............... ?

sk<u>ir</u>t	s<u>ee</u>n
<u>gar</u>den	h<u>ear</u>d

2 A: Do you like my .... b(oo)ts?
  B: I pref(er) the .... ones.

bl<u>ue</u>	gr<u>ee</u>n
<u>pur</u>ple	r<u>e</u>d

3 A: When did you l(o)se your .... ?
  B: L(a)st ....

<u>Mar</u>ch	s<u>ui</u>tcase
<u>Thur</u>sday	gui<u>tar</u>

4 A: What did he do when he s(aw) the .... ?
  B: He st(ar)ted to ....

scr<u>ea</u>m	l<u>au</u>gh
rep<u>or</u>t	maga<u>z</u>ine

5 A: It's his b(ir)thday on the ...., isn't it?
  B: Yes. I've b(ough)t him a .... TV.

p<u>or</u>table	f<u>our</u>th
n<u>ew</u>	th<u>ir</u>d

6 A: Where did your .... leave the c(ar)?
  B: It's p(ar)ked in the ....

d<u>augh</u>ter	<u>fa</u>ther
<u>car</u> park	str<u>ee</u>t

4 Listen and check your answers. ⊙━

When you have done this, listen again and repeat the conversations a line at a time.

5 Work in pairs and say the conversations together.

Unit 6 /æ/ & /ɑː/ and /ɪ/ & /iː/

Focus on /æ/ and /ɑː/

1 Some words are pronounced differently in different parts of England. For example, the words in the box are normally pronounced with /ɑː/ (as in d<u>ar</u>k and p<u>ar</u>k) by people from the south east of the country (area A on the map), but with /æ/ (as in c<u>a</u>t and s<u>a</u>t) by people from the north (area B on the map). ⊙━

bathroom	glasses	dance	ask	last	answer	passport
fast	after	past	path	afternoon		

Listen to these sentences and focus on the words that are given in the box. Do you think the speakers come from area A or B on the map?

1   Where's the bathroom, please?
2   I can't find my glasses.
3   Would you like to dance?
4   Ask him where he comes from?
5   I was there last week.
6   Can you answer the telephone, please?
7   Don't forget your passport.
8   You're driving too fast.
9   I'll do it after the football match.
10 It's five past eight.
11 There's a path down the garden.
12 She's arriving this afternoon.

Focus on /ɪ/ and /iː/

2   Repeat the words in the box.

India	river	sweets	Swedish	street	fourteen	knee
builder	British	teacher	milk	city	chicken	
Christmas	finger	Egypt	Easter	tea	stream	
a million						

3   Work in pairs. From the words in the box find two ... 0ᴛ

1 ... things to eat
2 ... numbers
3 ... things containing water
4 ... jobs
5 ... parts of the body

6 ... places where people live
7 ... holiday times
8 ... countries
9 ... nationalities
10 ... things to drink

4   Report your answers to the rest of the class like this:
       'sweets and chicken'
       'fourteen and a million'
Discuss any differences.

Unit 7 /ʌ/, /ʊ/ & /uː/ and /ɒ/ & /ɔː/

Focus on /ʌ/, /ʊ/ and /uː/

1 All the words in the box include the letter 'u'. How is it pronounced? Write the words in the table.

| include   customer   full |
| supermarket   June   gun |
| pull   Sunday   flu   put |
| push   number |

/ʌ/ e.g. sun	/ʊ/ e.g. would	/uː/ e.g. two

2 Repeat the words and check your answers. ⊙━

3 Work in pairs. Arrange these sentences into five two-line conversations. One is done for you.

     a) 6. & 2.   b) .... & ....   c) .... & ....   d) .... & ....   e) .... & ....

1   Where shall I put your luggage?
2   But I bought a new tube on Tuesday.
3   It's too hot. It's a lovely sunny day.
4   My uncle. Would you like me to introduce you?
5   It's from a really good cook book.
6   There isn't much toothpaste left.
7   In the boot. There's just a suitcase.
8   I think I'll put on my woollen jumper.
9   Who's that in the blue suit?
10   That onion soup was wonderful.

4 Repeat the conversations a line at a time and check your answers. Then work in pairs and say the conversations together. ⊙━

5 Underline all the /ʌ/, /ʊ/ and /uː/ sounds in the sentences. How many of each can you find? ⊙━

Focus on /ɒ/ and /ɔː/

6 Repeat these words. Notice the underlined vowels.

/ɒ/

ch<u>o</u>colate	<u>o</u>ffice
c<u>o</u>ffee	h<u>o</u>spital
d<u>o</u>g	

/ɔː/

w<u>a</u>lk	h<u>or</u>se
f<u>or</u>ty	d<u>au</u>ghter
dr<u>aw</u>	

7 Find someone in your class who ...

1 ... doesn't like chocolate.
2 ... can ride a horse.
3 ... doesn't drink coffee.
4 ... likes dogs.
5 ... is under forty.

6 ... walks to work.
7 ... has never stayed in hospital.
8 ... has a daughter.
9 ... works in an office.
10 ... can draw well.

Ask questions like this:
   Do you like chocolate?
   Can you ride a horse?
Report your answers to the rest of the class.

Unit 8   The long vowels /eɪ/, /aɪ/, /əʊ/ and /aʊ/

1 Repeat these words and notice the underlined vowel sounds.

/eɪ/	/aɪ/	/əʊ/	/aʊ/
d<u>ay</u>	cl<u>i</u>mb	ph<u>o</u>ne	p<u>ou</u>nd
br<u>ea</u>k	<u>i</u>ce	kn<u>ow</u>	n<u>ow</u>
ch<u>a</u>nge	f<u>igh</u>t	sm<u>o</u>ke	c<u>ou</u>nt
esc<u>a</u>pe	exc<u>i</u>ted	Oct<u>o</u>ber	m<u>ou</u>ntain

2 Work in pairs to complete the table. How many of these vowel sounds are there in the words in each line? The first line is done for you. **O━**

	/eɪ/	/aɪ/	/əʊ/	/aʊ/
1 snow face down coach slowly	1	0	3	1
2 neighbour delay age dry weigh				
3 road trousers mouth shave power				
4 drive polite type right brown				
5 although complaint round bowl main				
6 quite thousand silence high owe				

3 First cover up the story under the pictures. Look at these pictures and listen to the story. Say 'Stop!' when you hear a mistake and then say what is wrong. 0—

One morning last April, Joan was lying in bed when the doorbell rang. It was her friend, Dave, who invited her out for a picnic at the seaside. Later that day Jean left her flat and drove her car to the bus station to catch the bus. She was wearing a T-shirt and skirt as it was quite hot. As she sat on the bus she looked out of the door. The sun was shining. She saw a plane going over a forest and some horses in the fields. Before long she arrived at the river and met Steve. They went down to the beach and had their picnic next to a rock. They had sandwiches and crisps, and Steve painted a picture. They had a lovely day.

4 Work in pairs. Read the story and discuss the mistakes. Correct it like this:
'April' is wrong. It should be 'July'.
'Doorbell' is wrong. It should be 'phone'.

5 Cover up the written story again and retell the story from the pictures.

Unit 9 /eɪ/ & /e/ and /əʊ/ & /ɔː/

Focus on /eɪ/ and /e/

1 Look at the words in the box. Underline the vowels pronounced /eɪ/ (as in d<u>ay</u> and r<u>ai</u>n), and circle the vowels pronounced /e/ (as in r<u>e</u>d and s<u>ai</u>d).

potato	dentist	Belgium	November	seven	eight
sailor	radio	train	Asia	May	sweater	Spain
yellow	table	grey	head	helicopter	South America
bed	embassy	bread	television	dress	brain	station

2 Repeat the words and check your answers. 0—

3   Work in pairs. 'Potato' and 'bread' are both things to eat. Find more pairs in the words in the box in **1**.

4   Report your answers to the rest of the class.

Focus on /əʊ/ and /ɔː/

5   Repeat these words. Notice the underlined vowels.

/əʊ/

cl<u>o</u>thes	sm<u>o</u>ke	
sn<u>ow</u>	<u>o</u>ld	h<u>o</u>le
c<u>o</u>ld	cl<u>o</u>sed	
ph<u>o</u>ne box		

/ɔː/

c<u>or</u>ner	<u>au</u>tumn
dr<u>aw</u>ing	w<u>a</u>lking
d<u>augh</u>ter	b<u>a</u>ld
fl<u>oor</u>	w<u>ar</u>mly

6   Use as many of the words in **5** as you can to describe the pictures which follow.

7   What other words that include the sounds /əʊ/ or /ɔː/ can you use to describe the pictures?

Picture 1   Picture 2

Part 2 Consonants

Unit 10 /p/, /b/, /t/, /d/, /k/ and /g/

1 To make the sounds underlined at the beginning of these words, part of the mouth is completely closed and then the air behind it is suddenly released. Repeat the words.

/p/	/b/	/t/	/d/	/k/	/g/
pay	back	talk	dance	kind	give
park	buy	table	date	cook	gate
page	better	tourist	disco	coffee	guess
purple	borrow	tidy	dollar	colour	going
postman	business	tennis	different	kitchen	garden

2 The pictures show how the sounds are made. Which sounds are shown in (a), (b) and (c)? Each picture shows *two* sounds. **O─**

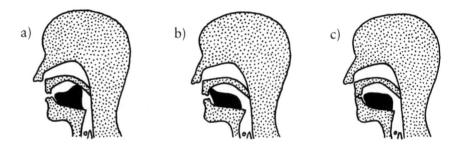

a)   b)   c)

3 Tom, Deborah, Kathy, Gary, Pam and Barbara are thinking about the presents they would like for their birthdays. Tom wants things that begin with the sound /t/, Deborah with the sound /d/, Kathy with the sound /k/, and so on. What presents do they each want? Make sentences like these: **O─**

Tom wants some trousers.
Deborah wants a dictionary.

Who wants most presents?
Who wants fewest presents?
Can you suggest some other presents they might like?

4 Repeat the words in box A. Then repeat the words in box B.

A
deep	dangerous	good
beautiful	boring	bad
colourful	comfortable	
patient	terrible	

B
dentist	doctor	garden
bed	cave	camera
cook	party	pain
tiger	television	town
teacher		

Work in pairs. Add words from A to words from B to find:

1 Something that is frightening.
(for example: a deep cave)
2 Something that is expensive.
3 Someone who does a good job.

4 Someone who does not do a good job.
5 Something you like.
6 Something you don't like.

Report your answers to the rest of the class.

Unit 11 /t/ & /d/ and /p/ & /b/

Focus on /t/ and /d/

1 Listen to these words. They all contain both the sounds /t/ and /d/. If the sound /t/ comes first, write *a*. If the sound /d/ comes first, write *b*. For example, if you heard the word 'advertise' you would write *b*; if you heard the word 'outside' you would write *a*. **0–ﻌ**

| Remember: | /t/... /d/ write *a*. | /d/... /t/ write *b*. |

1 ....   2 ....   3 ....   4 ....   5 ....   6 ....   7 ....   8 ....   9 ....   10 ....

2 Work in pairs. Arrange the sentences below into five two-line conversations. One is done for you.

a) *1 & 9* ....   b) ....   c) ....   d) ....   e) ....

1 What's twenty divided by two?
2 A taxi's too dear. Let's drive.
3 She's training to be a doctor.
4 What's the departure time?
5 What's your daughter doing now?

6 It's ten past ten.
7 Shall we take a taxi, or drive?
8 I didn't think it was too difficult.
9 Ten.
10 What did you think of the test today?

3 Repeat the conversations a line at a time and check your answers. Then work in pairs and say the conversations together. **0–ﻌ**

Focus on /p/ and /b/

4 Match the words on the left with the words on the right to describe what you can see in the pictures.

a pile of		pie
a book of		perfume
a basket of		pyjamas
a piece of		stamps
a portion of		pencils
a box of		chips
a packet of		shopping
a bar of		pears
a bag of		pasta
a pair of		biscuits
a bottle of		grapes
a bunch of		bricks
a plate of		soap

5 Repeat and check your answers. 🔑

6 Can you think of any other ways of completing the phrases on the left? The words you add must contain either the sound /p/ or /b/.

Unit 12　/s/, /z/, /f/, /v/, /θ/ and /ð/

1 To make the sounds underlined in these words, air is pushed through a narrow opening in the mouth. Repeat the words.

/s/	/z/	/f/	/v/	/θ/	/ð/
same	zoo	five	voice	thanks	this
sit	zebra	phone	very	thought	that
sister	easy	family	village	thief	those
single	amuse	February	visa	thirteen	their
Saturday	cause	photograph	visitor	Thursday	they

2 The pictures show how the sounds are made. Which sounds are shown in (a), (b) and (c)? 🔑

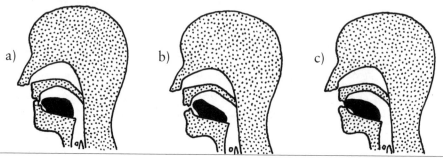

a)　　　　　　b)　　　　　　c)

3 Work in pairs. Discuss with your partner how to say these numbers.

1st (77) ... 2nd 3rd
443 5th 4,000
7/2/1975 4th 15/12/1657
3,000

13th Sept Thursday   Sept 14th Friday

4 Listen to these words. Do you hear (a) or (b)? Put a tick in the correct box.

	(a)		(b)			(a)		(b)			(a)		(b)	
1	sat	□	fat	□	6	few	□	view	□	11	bath	□	bars	□
2	fat	□	that	□	7	some	□	thumb	□	12	death	□	deaf	□
3	sing	□	thing	□	8	sort	□	thought	□	13	path	□	pass	□
4	say	□	they	□	9	few	□	zoo	□	14	that	□	sat	□
5	sink	□	think	□	10	fan	□	van	□	15	there	□	fair	□

5 Work in pairs. Look at the words labelled 1(a) and 1(b). Your partner should say one of the words SILENTLY to you. Try to decide which one is being said. You should answer, for example:
   'I think you said word (a).'
   or, if you can't decide,
   'Did you say "sat" or "fat"?'
Then continue for 2(a) and 2(b), and so on. Take it in turns to be 'hearer' and 'speaker'.

Unit 13 /θ/ & /ð/ and /v/, /f/ & /b/

Focus on /θ/ and /ð/

1 Repeat these sentences.

1 Three thirty.
2 The bathroom's through there.
3 They're brothers, aren't they?
4 When does it get there?
5 Is that Tom and David?
6 That's OK.

2   Work in pairs. Write the sentences in **1** in the spaces in these conversations. Then say the conversations together. 🔑

1   A: Where's the toilet?
    B: ....
    A: Thanks.
    B: ....

2   A: What time's the train to Doncaster?
    B: ....
    A: ....
    B: Ten twenty-three.

3   A: ....
    B: Yes, they're always together.
    A: ....
    B: That's right.

Focus on /v/, /f/ and /b/

3   Listen to these words. Do you hear (a) or (b)? Put a tick in the correct box. 🔑

	(a)		(b)			(a)		(b)	
1	bone	☐	phone	☐	6	boot	☐	foot	☐
2	boat	☐	vote	☐	7	build	☐	filled	☐
3	blood	☐	flood	☐	8	bye	☐	fly	☐
4	bet	☐	vet	☐	9	bridge	☐	fridge	☐
5	bill	☐	fill	☐	10	ball	☐	fall	☐

4   Work in pairs. Your partner should say one of the words in each pair SILENTLY to you. Try to decide which one is being said.

5   On the left are some of the things Beverly did today. On the right are the places where she did them. Work in pairs to ask and answer questions like this: 🔑

     A: Where did Beverly watch television?   B: In the living room.

She ...

watched television	in the bathroom.
bought some traveller's cheques	at a travel agent's.
booked a holiday	from the library.
bought a novel	on a bus.
delivered a birthday card	in the living room.
had a very long bath	from a bookshop.
borrowed some books	in the bank.
had a conversation with a bus driver	at a fruit and vegetable shop.
bought some bananas	to her neighbour.

Unit 14 /ʃ/, /tʃ/, /ʒ/ and /dʒ/

1 To make the sounds underlined in these words, the tongue is touching or close to the roof of the mouth. Repeat the words.

/ʃ/	/tʃ/	/ʒ/	/dʒ/
short	chair	decision	June
should	cheap	television	jump
shout	check	garage	jacket
shower	choose	pleasure	January
shopping	cheerful	usually	general

2 Work in pairs. Match the questions on the left with the answers on the right. Ask and answer like this:

> A: *Where would you usually* watch television?
> B: In the lounge.

a) watch television?   •   •   at a shoe shop.
b) arrange a holiday?   •   •   at a bank.
c) buy shoes?   •   •   at college.
d) wash up?   •   •   in the garage.
e) keep cheese?   •   •   at a newsagent's.
f) learn a foreign language?   •   •   in the kitchen.
g) catch a coach?   •   •   at a coach station.
h) cash a cheque?   •   •   at a travel agent's.
i) buy matches?   •   •   in the lounge.
j) keep a car?   •   •   in the fridge.

3 Repeat the words in the box.

peaches	sugar	orange juice	jam	chicken	cherries
porridge	champagne	fish	mushrooms	cabbage	
fresh vegetables	milk shake	cheese	chocolate	chips	

4 Work in pairs. Discuss whether the things in the box are good or bad to eat or drink when you want to lose weight.

5 Listen to this doctor talking to her patient. The patient has said he feels tired all the time and the doctor is now asking him about his diet. Put a tick next to the words in the box in **3** that you hear them talking about.

6 In pairs take the part of the doctor and patient, and discuss some of the other food and drink in the box in **3** in the same way.

Unit 15   /ʃ/ & /tʃ/ and /dr/ & /tr/

Focus on /ʃ/ and /tʃ/

1   The sound /ʃ/ is normally spelt 'sh' and the sound /tʃ/ 'ch'. However, in some words they do have different spellings. Listen to these words and decide how the underlined letters are pronounced. Tick the correct box.

	/ʃ/	/tʃ/		/ʃ/	/tʃ/
information	☐	☐	special	☐	☐
furniture	☐	☐	commercial	☐	☐
education	☐	☐	temperature	☐	☐
insurance	☐	☐	examination	☐	☐
suggestion	☐	☐	picture	☐	☐
profession	☐	☐	delicious	☐	☐
question	☐	☐	station	☐	☐

◄◄ **2**   Listen again. Repeat the words and check your answers. 🔑

Focus on /dr/ and /tr/

3   Repeat the words in the box. Concentrate on pronouncing the letters 'dr' and 'tr' correctly in each.

> street   traffic   drums   Austria   instruments   dress
> countries   train   wardrobe   travel   drive   Australia
> trumpet   dry   pedestrians

4   Work in pairs. Use the words in **3** to complete these sentences. Some are done for you. Then say the conversations together. 🔑

1   A: It's a really busy ....
   B: Yes, there's always a lot of *traffic*........ and ....

2   A: Which .... do you play?
   B: The .... and the *drums*........

3 A: What .... would you most like to visit?
   B: *Australia*.. and ....

4 A: Are you going to *drive*...........?
   B: No, I'll .... by ....

5 A: Is her .... *dry*............. yet?
   B: Yes, it's in the ....

Unit 16 /w/, /r/, /j/ and /l/

1 **Repeat these groups of words.**

/w/	/r/	/j/	/l/
week	radio	yes	last
west	really	year	less
would	river	young	learn
wallet	reason	yours	listen
white	recently	yellow	language

2 **Underline all the /w/ sounds in this conversation. Can you find any 'w' letters that are not pronounced /w/?**

A: What's the weather like?

B: Awful. It's wet and windy.

A: Shall we have a walk anyway?

B: Let's wait twenty minutes.

Repeat the conversation a sentence at a time. Then say the conversation in pairs.

3 **Underline all the /j/ sounds in this conversation. Can you find any 'y' letters that are not pronounced /j/? Can you find any /j/ sounds that are not written with the letter 'y'?**

A: I had an interview yesterday.

B: Where?

A: At the Daily News.

B: Did you get the job?

A: I don't know yet.

Repeat. Then say it in pairs.

4 Underline all the /r/ sounds in this conversation. Can you find any 'r' letters that are not pronounced /r/? 〇ᴎ

A: Did you remember to ring Ray?

B: I tried three times on Friday.

A: He was probably at work.

B: You're probably right. I'll try again tomorrow.

Repeat. Then say it in pairs.

5 Listen to this conversation. Bob is asking Sarah about her holiday. When you hear the answers to the questions on the left, write the answers in column A. Use words from the boxes. Some are done for you. 〇ᴎ

	A	B	
Where?	Sweden		Italy, Bulgaria, the USA, Sweden
Who with?			with family, alone, with a friend
Hotel?	clean		clean, comfortable, swimming pool, large, old, quiet, uncomfortable
Things to do?			swimming, walking, yachting, windsurfing, sleeping, films
Weather?	cool		lovely, cloudy, wet, cool, windy, dry, usually hot, cold

6 Choose words from the boxes on the right to write notes about an imaginary holiday. Write them in column B. Then work in pairs and talk about your holiday with your partner.

Unit 17 /w/ & /v/ and /r/ & /l/

Focus on /w/ and /v/

1 For this task, first cover up the sentences on the right. Listen to these five sentences. How many /v/ sounds do you hear in each? Write your answer in the box.

1 ☐   I've only got twelve.
2 ☐   She works hard every day.
3 ☐   We had to drive up the pavement to avoid him.
4 ☐   I've lost my wallet, traveller's cheques and visa.
5 ☐   We're having visitors over the weekend.

2 Uncover the sentences and check your answers. Listen again and repeat the sentences. **O—π**

3 Now you will hear five more sentences. How many /w/ sounds do you hear in each? Write your answer in the box.

1 ☐   What's this one over here?
2 ☐   Was every piece of furniture made of wood?
3 ☐   It's quite warm for November.
4 ☐   They're having just a quiet wedding next Wednesday.
5 ☐   It was very wet last week, wasn't it?

4 Uncover the sentences and check your answers. Listen again and repeat the sentences. **O—π**

Focus on /r/ and /l/

5 Which of the adjectives in box A can be used to describe the nouns in box B? **O—π**

Work in pairs. Discuss your answers with your partner and be ready to report back to the rest of the class. Report back your answers like this:

You might say 'a rich uncle', *but probably not* 'a rich letter'.

A		B	
slippery rich musical electronic horrible dangerous difficult Australian clean private lovely favourite		river football brother uncle road calculator instrument flower problem letter bathroom building	

Unit 18 /m/, /n/ and /ŋ/

1 To make the sounds underlined in these words, part of the mouth is completely closed and air is allowed to pass through the nose. Repeat the words.

/m/	/n/	/ŋ/
many	name	bring
make	near	long
mend	nobody	spring
milk	news	strong
mouth	number	finger

2 Write the sentences from the box next to the pictures to describe what Nick is doing in each. Then repeat the sentences and check your answers. ⚷

He's ironing.
He's washing up.
He's painting.
He's singing.
He's playing tennis.
He's shopping.
He's studying English grammar.
He's cooking.
He's gardening.
He's listening to music.

1

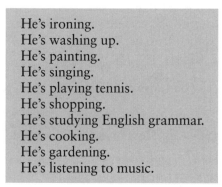

2

....

3

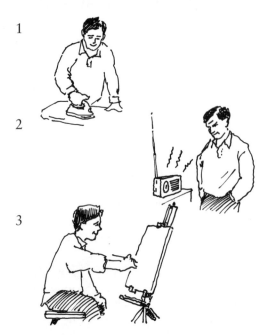

....

....

4 ....

5 ....

6 ....

7 ....

8 ....

9 ....

10 ....

3 Work in pairs. Study the pictures for one minute and then close your book. Try to remember what Nick likes doing and what he doesn't like doing. Report to your partner like this: O—ϗ

He likes ironing.

He doesn't like listening to music.

Your partner will check your answers.

4 Martha has made a list of things she wants to do in town today. Work in pairs and decide where she needs to go. Choose from the places given in the box. Then report your decisions to the class.

> cinema   bank
> supermarket   chemist
> department store   newsagent
> restaurant   Indian Embassy

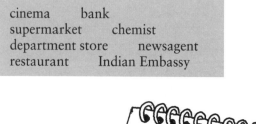

Arrange visa for
holiday in India.

Get money.
Do shopping.
Buy handbag,
perfume, sunglasses,
computer magazine.
See new James Bond film.
Have dinner with Norma.

Part 3 Consonant clusters

Unit 19 Consonant letters and consonant sounds

1 A *consonant cluster* is found when two or more *consonant sounds* come together. For example, the word 'spell' begins with the consonant cluster /sp/, and the word 'against' ends with the consonant cluster /nst/.

2 Underline the parts of the words where there are two or more *consonant letters* together. The first three are done for you. ⊙┓

	Number of consonant letters	Number of consonant sounds		Number of consonant letters	Number of consonant sounds
1 blood	2	2	7 light		
2 jump	2	2	8 next		
3 ticket	2	1	9 there		
4 tablet			10 report		
5 dollar			11 film		
6 chair			12 street		

Complete the first column with the number of consonant letters you have underlined.

Complete the second column with the number of consonant sounds you have underlined. What do you notice about the number of consonant letters and sounds?

3 Work in pairs and complete this table. The first two boxes are done for you. 'Clock' *begins* with the consonant cluster /kl/; there is no word in English beginning with the consonant cluster /km/. The pictures on the right may help you to complete *some* of the boxes. ⊙┓

	/l/	/m/	/r/
/k/	clock	x	cross
/d/			
/g/			
/p/			
/s/			
/t/			

4 In pairs, say to each other the words you have written. Underline any words you find difficult to say.

5 Look at this word chain.

Each word begins with a consonant cluster. *One* of the consonant sounds is the same as in the consonant cluster beginning the previous word. Make similar word chains around the class.

If you give a wrong word or can't think of a word you are out of the chain. Don't repeat words.

Unit 20 Consonant clusters at the beginning of words

1 Repeat these words. Pay attention to the pronunciation of the sounds that are underlined.

1	blue	3	cloudy	5	quite	7	practise
	black		clearly		quietly		pronunciation
	blood		clean		quickly		press
	blanket		clock		quarter		pretty
	blouse		clothes		question		programmes
2	bring	4	cross	6	played		
	bread		cry		please		
	Britain		crash		plenty		
	bridge		crack		plate		
	brother		crisps		plug		

2 Repeat the sentences *on the right*. They include some of the words from the lists in **1**.

What did Sue have for Christmas? •   • Just bread and crisps.
How can I speak English better? •   • A blue blouse.
What do we need from the •   • Quite cloudy.
 supermarket?
What should I take on my holiday •   • Practise your pronunciation.
 to Iceland?
What's the weather like? •   • Plenty of warm clothes.

3 Work in pairs. Match these questions on the left with the answers on the right and say the short conversations together. O—ᴋ

28

4   Repeat these words. Pay attention to the pronunciation of the sounds that are <u>underlined</u>.

8 <u>sl</u>eepy   10 <u>st</u>art   12 <u>tr</u>y
   <u>sl</u>owly   <u>st</u>amps   <u>tr</u>ouble
   <u>sl</u>im   <u>st</u>ill   <u>tr</u>ee
   <u>sl</u>ippery   <u>st</u>and   <u>tr</u>ain
   <u>sl</u>ippers   <u>st</u>ation   <u>tr</u>ousers

9 <u>sp</u>ill   11 <u>thr</u>ee
   <u>sp</u>eaking   <u>thr</u>ough
   <u>sp</u>orts   <u>thr</u>ow
   <u>sp</u>ade   <u>thr</u>illers
   <u>sp</u>elling   <u>thr</u>oat

5   Complete these conversations with words from groups (1) to (12).

6   Work in pairs and say the conversations together.

Unit 21 More on consonant clusters at the beginning of words

1 Listen to these sentences. They include a word *either* from box A *or* from box B. Write the word you hear in the spaces. The first one is done for you. **O⊸**

A

clock	brought
grow	plane
driver	true
play	stay
spend	sport

B

lock	bought
go	pain
diver	two
pay	say
send	sort

1 Is the _clock_............... broken?
2 They'll .... much higher than that.
3 He used to be a postman, but now he's a ....
4 Shall we .... now or later?
5 How much money did she ....?

6 How many have you ....?
7 The .... was terrible.
8 Are you sure it's ....?
9 Did you .... two weeks or three?
10 What .... do you like best?

2 Work in pairs. Say the sentences to your partner. Complete them with either a word from box A or a word from box B. Your partner should try to decide which box the word is from.

3 Write the words in the box in the spaces next to the pictures. Then repeat the words. **O⊸**

a ski suit	a frying pan	a plate	a clock	skis	gloves
a scarf	a sleeping bag	a spade	a dress	a sweater	
flippers	slippers	a swimming costume		swimming trunks	

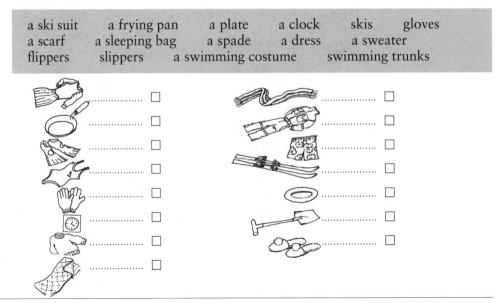

4 Look at the pictures and listen. You will hear two people talking about what to pack for *a skiing holiday*. Put a tick in the box next to the picture when you hear it mentioned. **0⟶**

5 Work in pairs. Make similar conversations about: (1) a camping holiday, (2) a holiday by the sea in a warm country.

Here are some phrases to help you:

Shall I take a/my …?　　　Yes, take that/those.
What about my …?　　　　No, you won't need your …

Don't forget to take your …
You might need your/a …

Unit 22　Consonant clusters at the end of words

1 Many English words end in the sound 'n' followed by another consonant. Listen to these words. Some of them end either in the *sounds* /n/+/s/, /n/+/t/ or /n/+/d/. *If they do*, write them in the table. *If they don't*, miss them out. The first three are done for you. **0⟶**

/n/+/s/	/n/+/t/	/n/+/d/
since	want	friend

◄◄ **2** Listen again. Repeat the words and check your answers. **0⟶**

3 Complete these conversations with words from the table. Then work in pairs and say the conversations together. **0⟶**

4 Repeat the words in the box.

elephant	adult	pleased	beetle	waist	wasp	child
fox	toast	yourself	terrible	amused	beans	ankle
wrist	tongue	orange	depressed	parents	boyfriend	
ant	milk	chips	chest			

5 Work in pairs. From the words in the box find some ... O—

1 ...things you can eat or drink.   4 ...people.
2 ...animals.   5 ...ways people feel.
3 ...parts of the body.

6 Report your answers to the rest of the class.

Unit 23   More on consonant clusters at the end of words

1 Repeat the words in the box. Notice the consonant clusters at the end of each word. In some of these words a very short vowel sound is sometimes put between the consonants. For example, 'special' might be pronounced /speʃl/ or /speʃəl/.

trouble	terrible	examination	eleven	special	hospital
cousin	button	middle	bicycle	listen	chemical
bottle	happen				

2 Work in pairs. Write words from the box in **1** in the spaces to complete these conversations.

1 A: Where's your ....?
   B: She's in ....
   A: What's the ....?
   B: She fell off her ....

2 A: When's the ....?
   B: At ....
   A: How do you feel?
   B: ....

3 A: What's in this ....?
   B: A ....
   A: What's it for?
   B: Something ....!

4 A: Press that ....
   B: This one in the ....?
   A: Yes.
   B: What'll ....?
   A: Just ....

3 Listen and check your answers. O—

◄◄ ▭ **4**   Listen again and repeat the conversations a line at a time. Then say the
conversations with a partner.

5   Ask your partner these questions and note their answers. Pay particular attention
to the pronunciation of the consonant clusters underlined.

1 Which of these subjects did you like best at school?	Physi<u>cs</u> Ma<u>ths</u> Chemi<u>stry</u>
2 Which of these colours do you like best?	Pur<u>pl</u>e Ora<u>ng</u>e Pi<u>nk</u>
3 Which of these jobs would you rather have?	Journali<u>st</u> Arti<u>st</u> Politi<u>cian</u>
4 Which of these places would you rather work in?	A hos<u>pit</u>al A ba<u>nk</u> A restaura<u>nt</u>
5 Which of these countries would you rather live in for the rest of your life?	Egy<u>pt</u> Thaila<u>nd</u> Fra<u>nce</u>

6   Report your findings to the rest of the class.

Unit 24 Consonant clusters in the middle of words

1   Look at the consonant clusters underlined in the middle of these words. Can you
also find them at the *beginning* and at the *end* of words in English? Complete the
left side of the table with a tick (✓) or cross (✗) and, if you can, give an example
word for each. The first two are done for you. ⊙⟲

Beginning	Middle	End
✓ (stop) ✗	cu<u>st</u>omer seve<u>nt</u>een Dece<u>mb</u>er shou<u>ld</u>er A<u>pr</u>il co<u>mp</u>any bla<u>nk</u>et e<u>nv</u>elope	✓ (last) ✓ (went)

2 Repeat these words. Pay attention to the consonant sounds underlined.

> aero<u>pl</u>ane   e<u>x</u>ercise   quie<u>tl</u>y   pa<u>ss</u>port   pra<u>ct</u>ical   hu<u>sb</u>and
> ho<u>sp</u>ital   pain<u>t</u>ing   boy<u>fr</u>iend   ta<u>x</u>i   a<u>ppl</u>y   ra<u>sp</u>berry
> har<u>dl</u>y   a<u>fr</u>aid   busine<u>ssm</u>an   lou<u>dl</u>y   mou<u>nt</u>ain   do<u>ct</u>or
> a<u>tl</u>as   adverti<u>sem</u>ent

3 Work in pairs. Choose words from the box in **2** to complete these sentences. The word you choose for each sentence should contain the sound shown. The first one is done for you. **O─ӄ**

1 /sp/   Someone's stolen my *passport*........!
2 /dl/   She sang the song very ....
3 /ks/   I went to see her by ....
4 /tl/   Play your records .... The baby's asleep.
5 /zb/   Bill's her new ....
6 /nt/   It costs a lot nowadays to buy a good ....
7 /sm/   He's a very successful ....
8 /kt/   She left her old job and now she wants to be a ....
9 /pl/   You can travel from Paris to Rome by ....
           in less than two hours.
10 /fr/   Her .... brings her flowers every day.

4 Repeat the words in the box.

> April   library   wardrobe   Oslo   apple pie   chocolates
> biscuits   toaster   December   tape recorder   hospital
> post office   Bombay   computer   cornflakes   bookshop
> October   armchair   bookshelf   London

5 Work in pairs. From the words in the box find some ... **O─ӄ**

1 ... cities.
2 ... months.
3 ... pieces of furniture.

4 ... things to eat.
5 ... things that use electricity.
6 ... buildings.

6 Report your answers to the rest of the class like this:
    'There are three cities – Oslo, Bombay and London.'

Unit 25 Consonant clusters across words

In this unit you will practise some of the consonant clusters that are found when a word beginning with a consonant follows a word ending with a consonant. For example, in 'breakfast cereal'.

1 Match each word on the left with one of the words on the right. One is done for you.

orange	•	•	time
arrival	•	•	music
capital	•	•	juice
classical	•	•	city

film	•	•	handed
girl	•	•	friend
left	•	•	television
portable	•	•	star

2 Listen. You will hear the most likely answers. Repeat the phrases and compare them with your answers. If you have any different answers discuss them with your teacher. 0⟍

3 Repeat the words in each box before listening to the conversations.

1
like them	think they're
that's very	it's true

a)

A: Do like them?
B: I think they're excellent.
A: That's very kind of you.
B: Really. It's true.

2
is this	this correct
and this	don't know

b)

A: Is this correct?
B: Those two are.
A: And this one?
B: I don't know.

3
last Saturday	I've missed
they'll be	next February

c)

A: When was it?
B: Last Saturday.
A: Oh, no. I've missed it.
B: They'll be back next February.

4	this morning John's borrowed
	got keys keys for we'd better

d)

A: It was there this morning.
B: Perhaps John's borrowed it.
A: He hasn't got keys for it.
B: Then we'd better call the police.

4 Match the conversations and the pictures in **3**. 0–

5 Work in pairs and say the conversations together.

Unit 26   More on consonant clusters across words

When the *same* consonant sound ends a word and starts the next word, for example in 'a team meeting' the consonant is usually only pronounced once, but slightly longer than usual.

1 Repeat the word in column 1, then the word in column 2, and then repeat the two words together.

1	2	3
team	meeting	She was wearing her .... at the party.
some	money	We lost the match ....
red	dress	.... came to see us yesterday.
bad	dream	They had a .... after the game.
it	takes	Is there .... for the party?
one	nil	A .... woke me up.
five	visitors	There's .... in my purse.
enough	food	.... five minutes.

2 Work in pairs. Write the phrases (e.g. 'team meeting') from columns 1 and 2 in the sentences in 3. Then say the sentences to your partner. 0–

3 Sometimes, when two or more consonant sounds occur together across words, one of the sounds changes its pronunciation or may even be nearly missed out. This happens especially to /t/ and /d/. Listen to these examples. Notice how the final /t/ and /d/ change.

last – last Saturday   just – just look

next – next February   and – and this

4 Listen and write the missing word in the spaces in these sentences. **O─**

1 It's .... today.

2 I'm really .... to see you again.

3 Is .... the man?

4 You can .... me at home.

5 She wasn't angry. In .... she was happy about it.

6 Will you .... me soon?

7 This is my .... Tom.

8 I .... do it.

5 Listen again and repeat the sentences. Notice the change in the last sound of the words you have written.

6 Work in pairs. Underline the consonant clusters in these sentences. **O─**

1 That's true.   6 Can you come tomorrow?
2 I don't know yet.   7 Can I have some more?
3 Help yourself.   8 Thanks very much.
4 It's very pretty.   9 But it's so expensive.
5 Please try.

7 Work in pairs. Sort the sentences into three three-line conversations and write the numbers of the sentences in the correct order in the spaces. One is done for you. Then say the conversations together. **O─**

a) 4.... .9... 1.....   b) ....   c) ....

Part 4 Stress and rhythm

Unit 27   Syllables and stress

1   Words can be divided into SYLLABLES. For example:

farm   has one syllable
be-gin   has two syllables
com-put-er   has three syllables
in-tell-ig-ent   has four syllables

How many syllables do these words have? Write your answers in the spaces. One is done for you.

furniture 3....   bought ....   blackboard ....   examination ....

remember ....   collect ....   anybody ....   please ....

grandmother ....   impossible ....   electricity ....   rabbit ....

directions ....   goodbye ....

2   Listen and check your answers. 0–ᴀ

3   Each word has one syllable that is STRESSED. The other syllables in the word are UNSTRESSED. In Part 4, stressed syllables will be marked by big circles, and unstressed syllables by small circles. These circles will be placed over the vowel sound in each syllable. For example:

   ◯   ○◯   ○ ◯○   ○ ◯○ ○
 farm   begin   computer   intelligent

Show the stressed and unstressed syllables in the same way in the words in **1**. For example:

   ◯ ○ ○
 furniture

4   Listen again to the words given in **1**. Repeat the words and check your answers. 0–ᴀ

5 Here are the English names of some capital cities. How many syllables are there in each name? Show which syllables are stressed. 🔑

Budapest

Bangkok

Madrid

Moscow

Jakarta

Lima

Unit 28   Patterns of stress in words

1 Four of the words in each of the lists below have the stress pattern shown and one has a different pattern. This is the *odd one out*. Before listening to the words, work in pairs and try to find the odd one out in each list.

1 ○◯   above, chicken, postpone, guitar, correct

2 ◯○   under, dirty, handsome, Japan, reason

3 ○◯○   exciting, tomorrow, November, injection, telephone

4 ◯○○   policeman, cinema, yesterday, politics, overcoat

5 ○○◯○   unemployment, competition, supermarket, information, immigration

2 Repeat the words and check your answers. 🔑

3   *Two* of the words in each of the sentences below have two syllables. Write ⬤ ○ or ○ ⬤ to show their stressed and unstressed syllables. One sentence has been done for you. Then repeat the sentences and check your answers. **⊙⇥**

A single or return?

I was hoping to invite you.

I'm a stranger here myself.

I'll be busy, I'm afraid.

Have you ever been abroad?

I'd like a ticket to Madrid.

Is the station far away?

I went to Brazil in April.

4   Work in pairs. Draw lines to match the sentences. Make four two-line conversations. One is done for you. Then say the conversations together. **⊙⇥**

Unit 29   More practice; stress patterns in numbers

1   How many syllables do these words have? Write your answer in the space. One is done for you. When you have finished, repeat the words and check your answers. **⊙⇥**

economics ..4...   Zimbabwe ....   diplomat ....   July ....
Chinese ....   biology ....   Arabic ....   Peru ....   August ....
photographer ....   Norwegian ....   Germany ....   accountant ....
chemistry ....   September ....

2   Work in pairs. Use the words in **1** to complete these conversations. Choose a word to match the stress shown. Then say the conversations together. **⊙⇥**

1 A: What does she do?
             ○ ⬤ ○
    B: She's a(n) ....

2 A: When are you going on holiday?
   B: In ....

3 A: I liked history at school.
   B: My favourite subject was ....

4 A: Do you speak Swedish?
   B: Yes, but I don't speak .... very well.

5 A: Where are you flying to?
   B: First to France and then on to ....

---

3 Listen to these sentences. Put a circle round the numbers you hear. 𝅘

1 11.14   11.40   4 17   70
2 15   50   5 £2.18   £2.80
3 16   60   6 £19   £90

4 If you are not sure if someone has said 30 or 13, 40 or 14, and so on, you should ask them to repeat. These conversations show you how. Listen.

A: He'll be thirty tomorrow.

B: I'm sorry. Did you say thirty or thirteen?

A: Thirty.

A: I live at number fourteen.

B: I'm sorry. Did you say forty or fourteen?

A: Fourteen.

5 Listen again and repeat the conversations a line at a time.

6 Work in pairs to make similar conversations starting with these sentences.

1 That will be £30, please.   3 To get to the theatre, catch bus 80.
2 Turn to page 17.   4 I'll see you at 3.15.

Unit 30   Finding out about stress patterns

1   Word stress in English is complicated, but it is possible to learn some simple rules.
Write *Noun*, *Verb* or *Adjective* after these words. Some are done for you.

carry *V*.....   famous *A*....   daughter *N*....   husband ....   forget ....
lovely ....   yellow ....   prefer ....   frighten ....   kitchen ....
ugly ....   mountain ....

2   Listen to the words in **1** and put ◯ over the stressed syllable and ◦ over the
unstressed syllable in each word. **0⊸**

3   Now complete these sentences with the words in the box to give you some simple
rules about two-syllable words in English. **0⊸**

Most .... and .... are stressed on	nouns
the first syllable. Some .... are stressed on	verbs
the first syllable and others on the second.	adjectives

4   If you're not sure of the stress pattern in a word, you could look in a dictionary.
Most dictionaries show stress. Usually they have a ' sign before the most stressed
syllable. You can normally work out where the stress goes even if you don't
understand the phonetics.
Write these words in the table. The first is done for you.

motorbike	/ˈməʊtəbaɪk/	across	/əˈkrɒs/
museum	/mjuːˈzɪəm/	ambulance	/ˈæmbjʊləns/
photograph	/ˈfəʊtəgrɑːf/	suggestion	/səˈdʒestʃən/
machine	/məˈʃiːn/	professor	/prəˈfesə/
July	/dʒʊˈlaɪ/	perhaps	/pəˈhæps/
garden	/ˈgɑːdn/	also	/ˈɔːlsəʊ/

◯ ◦	◦ ◯	◯ ◦ ◦	◦ ◯ ◦
		motorbike	

5   Repeat the words and check your answers. **0⊸**

6   Take two pieces of paper. From your coursebook, list ten words which have two
or more syllables. Write the list on both pieces of paper. Give one list to another
member of your class. Both of you can then mark stress on the words. Compare
the stress patterns you have marked. If they are different, check the answer in a
dictionary or with your teacher.

Unit 31   Pronouncing unstressed syllables

1   When they are in an unstressed syllable, many vowels are pronounced /ə/.
In the words below, the stressed syllable has a circle over it, and vowels
pronounced /ə/ are underlined. Listen.

about   cust<u>o</u>mer   pr<u>o</u>fess<u>or</u>

2   Do the same for these words. Show the syllable with the main stress with ◯,
unstressed syllables with ○ and underline vowels pronounced /ə/. The first one is
done for you.

1 answ<u>er</u>   5 Australian   9 woman

2 important   6 distant   10 computer

3 calculator   7 weather   11 American

4 visitor   8 mirror   12 pregnant

3   Repeat the words and check your answers. ⊙╥

4   Words with more than one syllable that end in '-er', '-or', '-(i)an', '-man' and
'-ant' are usually pronounced with /ə/ in the last syllable. Repeat this list of jobs.

doctor	actor	photographer	teacher	hairdresser
optician	electrician	fireman	policewoman	shop assistant

5   Work in pairs. Decide who you think earns more money. Then report your
answers to the rest of the class.

1   A doctor or a policewoman?

2 A teacher or a fireman?

3 A photographer or an electrician?

4 A hairdresser or a shop assistant?

5 An actor or an optician?

Unit 32 Rhythm

1 Some very common words in English have two pronunciations, sometimes called their STRONG and WEAK forms. Listen to the strong and weak forms of the words 'of', 'to' and 'and'. This table shows how they are pronounced.

	Strong form	Weak form	
'of'	/ɒv/	/əv/ or /ə/	A tin of tomatoes.
'to'	/tuː/	/tə/	I'm going to town.
'and'	/ænd/	/ənd/ or /ən/	David and Susan.

The weak forms of these words all include the sound /ə/. The weak forms are much more commonly used than the strong forms. The strong forms are used only when the word has some special emphasis or is said on its own.

2 Listen to these sentences. Write 'of', 'to' or 'and' in each space.

1 A bottle .... milk.
2 I'll go .... see.
3 I've nothing .... say.
4 A hundred .... forty.
5 I'm going .... London.
6 I have .... go.

7 A piece .... cake.
8 The first .... October.
9 My mother .... father.
10 I've lots .... do.
11 A type .... bread.
12 What's six .... eight?

◀◀ ▣ 3 Listen again. Repeat the sentences and check your answers. ⚷

4 Which of these types of food go together? Complete each phrase with a word from the box.

fish and ....
bread and ....
cheese and ....
coffee and ....
apple pie and ....

biscuits	cream	butter
chips	cake	

5 Repeat the phrases and check your answers. Pronounce 'and' as /ən/. ○━

6 Talk about what you are going to eat. You should add a similar phrase when it is your turn to speak.

A: I'm really hungry. When I get home I'm going to have some bread and butter.
B: I'm going to have bread and butter, and fish and chips.
C: I'm going to have bread and butter, fish and chips, and apple pie and cream.
D: ......

7 Think of some more phrases like this that describe foods that go together, and do the task again.

Unit 33 More on rhythm

1 Repeat these sentences. Compare their rhythm.

◯ ◦ ◯   ◯ ◦ ◦ ◯   ◦◯ ◦ ◦ ◯
1 Black or white?   2 Where are you from?   3 I go there a lot.

2 Listen to these sentences. Are they like 1, 2 or 3? One is done for you. ○━
Then listen again and repeat.

2.... What did he say?	•	• Five pounds an hour. ....
.... Shall we dance?	•	• I'll call the police. ....
.... What do you earn?	•	• He told me to rest. ....
.... Here is your change.	•	• Thanks very much. ....
.... Where's it gone?	•	• On the roof. ....
.... Give me your purse.	•	• Yes, of course. ....

3 Work in pairs. Draw lines to match the sentences and then say the six short conversations together. ○━

4 Work in pairs. One should be A and the other B. Repeat each conversation and then continue the dialogue in the same way. Try to continue with the same rhythm as on the recording. In this exercise the syllables to be stressed are in bold letters.

1 When shall we meet?
   A: **Shall** we meet on **Thurs**day?
   B: I **can't** on Thursday.
   A: **Well, how** about Friday?
   B: I **can't** on Friday.
   A: **Well, how** about Saturday?
   B: I **can't** on Saturday.
   A: **Well, how** about **Sun**day?
   B: ......

2 When shall we go?
   A: **Shall** we go in **Jan**uary?
   B: I **can't** in January.
   A: **Well, how** about in **Feb**ruary?
   B: I **can't** in February.
   A: **Well, how** about in **March**?
   B: ......

3 What shall we have to eat?
   A: **Why** don't we have **fish**?
   B: I **don't like** fish.
   A: **Well, why** don't we have **chicken**?
   B: I **don't like** chicken.
   A: **Well, why** don't we have **beef**?
   B: ......

5 Work in pairs and write one more similar conversation called:
       'Where shall we go?'
   Practise it and then perform it for the rest of the class.

Unit 34 Rhythm and moving stress

1 Look at this picture of the students in an English language class. Their jobs are
   written next to them. Find out their nationalities. Listen to a teacher talking
   about the class and write words from the box in the spaces.

dentist ....

journalist ....

diplomat ....

doctor ....

businessman ....

teacher ....

actress ....

farmer ....

Chinese
Swedish
Portuguese
Spanish
Taiwanese
Japanese
Italian
Norwegian

2 Listen again to some of the words used by the teacher. Draw a large circle over the stressed syllable and a small circle over the unstressed syllables in each word. One is done for you. **O–π**

○ ○ ◯
Japanese　　Swedish　　Chinese　　Spanish

Taiwanese　　Norwegian　　Italian　　Portuguese

◄◄ **3** Listen again and repeat the words.

4 In some words, stress can move to a different syllable. This usually happens if another stressed syllable follows the word. For example: **O–π**

○ ○ ◯　　　　　　◯ ○ ○　　◯ ○
He's Japanese.　　but　　He's a Japanese doctor.

Which of the other nationality words have this moving stress? Listen and write a tick or a cross.

1 Japanese ✓....　　　　5 Taiwanese ....
2 Swedish ....　　　　6 Norwegian ....
3 Chinese ....　　　　7 Italian ....
4 Spanish ....　　　　8 Portuguese ....

5 Many numbers also have this MOVING STRESS. Listen to this conversation.

A: Where does Jim live?

◯　　◯
B: Lime Road.

A: What number does Jim live at?

◯ ○ ◯
B: Twenty-two.

A: What's Jim's address?

◯ ○ ○　　◯　　◯
B: Twenty-two Lime Road.

◄◄ **6** Listen again and repeat the conversation a line at a time.

7   Work in pairs to make similar questions and answers using these pictures.

Part 5 Sounds in connected speech

Unit 35 Slow speech and connected speech

It is sometimes difficult to understand English speakers when they are talking at normal speed – which often sounds fairly fast! One reason for this is that the pronunciation of some words is different when they are said on their own, or in slow, careful speech, from when they are used in CONNECTED SPEECH. The units in Part 5 help you to *understand* and to *practise* connected speech in English.

Understanding sentences in connected speech

1 Listen to these sentences and write them down. They are said at normal speed. Some of the words are given. The first one is done for you. 🔑

1 *It's over* .... there.
2 .... five ....
3 .... seven.
4 .... do ....?
5 .... soon ....
6 .... think ....
7 .... good.
8 .... got ....
9 .... said ....
10 .... do .... tomorrow.

2 Before you check your answers, listen to the sentences again. This time they are part of short conversations. If there were any in **1** that you didn't understand, try to work out what they mean from the *context*. 🔑

Understanding questions in connected speech

3 Read these answers to questions. Then listen to the questions and match them with the answers. Write 1 to 8 in the spaces under the pictures. One is done for you. 🔑

a) *8*....   b) ....   c) ....

49

d) ....   e) ....   f) ....

g) ....   h) ....

◄◄ ▭ **4** Listen again. Write the questions in the spaces in the bubbles. ⊶

▭ **5** Listen to the conversations and repeat them a line at a time.

6 Work in pairs. Say the conversations with your partner. Try to say them at normal speed.

Unit 36 Common words and phrases in connected speech

▭ **1** Some very common words are pronounced differently in slow and in normal speech. Decide what word might be missing from these sentences. (One word is missing from each space.) Then listen and write the word you hear. ⊶

1 Two .... three.
2 Call .... ambulance.
3 On .... off.
4 John .... Ann.
5 Some .... over here.

6 It's a packet .... biscuits.
7 .... they coming?
8 It's a container .... ice cream.
9 He wants .... computer.
10 Some .... already paid.

◄◄ ▭ **2** Listen again and repeat the sentences.

3   This table shows how the words you wrote in **1** can be pronounced. Why are
there two pronunciations of 'are', 'of' and 'or'? ⚷

	Words
/ə/	are, a, or, of
/əv/	of, have
/ər/	or, are
/ən/	and, an

(Note: The sound /ə/ is pronounced as in <u>a</u>go or driv<u>er</u>.)

4   Listen to these conversations. Write the missing parts in the spaces. Use the usual
written form of the words and phrases that you hear. Some are done for you. ⚷

1 A: ....
   B: *Yes, what can I do for you?*

2 A: *What is it?* ....
   B: ....

3 A: *What time is it?* ....
   B: ....

4 A: ....
   B: ....

5 A: ....
   B: ....

5   Features of connected speech are sometimes included in written English. This is
especially true in the words of pop songs. What do you think the marked words
in these lines from pop songs would be in slow, careful English? Write your
answers in the spaces. ⚷

1 I don't <u>wanna</u> say that I've been unhappy with you.   ....
2 All you've <u>gotta</u> do is call.   ....
3 'Cos I'm happy just to dance with you.   ....
4 I'm <u>gonna getcha</u> … I'm <u>gonna meetcha</u>.   ....
5 <u>You gotta teach 'em 'bout</u> freedom.   ....

Unit 37 Linking words together: Consonant + Vowel

In connected speech, words are often linked together smoothly without a break
between them. This unit practises linking words that end in a *consonant sound*
with a word that begins with a *vowel sound*.

1 Repeat these sentences. Make sure you link the words together as shown.

1 Look at these pictures.
2 An American car.
3 One or two friends.
4 I'll have these instead.
5 She's from Australia.
6 He's quite old.
7 It's upstairs.
8 Tom used to live here.
9 I'm going in April.
10 The shop isn't open yet.

2 Work in pairs. Say the sentences to each other. Check that your partner is linking the words together.

3 Work in pairs. Match the words on the left to the words on the right. One is done for you.

1 a crowd	of hours
2 a map	of the world
3 a box	of flowers
4 a bunch	of drawers
5 a block	of cake
6 a couple	of matches
7 a piece	of people
8 a chest	of flats

4 Repeat the phrases and check your answers. Make sure you link the consonant sound at the end of the first part with the vowel sound at the beginning of the second.

5 Work in pairs. Make a list of what you 'put up', 'put out', etc. Use words from this box and try to think of more.

the radio the grass the cooker your coat a light a car
an umbrella golf a bus your clothes

1 put up ....
2 put out ....
3 put on ....
4 take off ....
5 take up ....
6 turn off ....
7 turn up ....
8 get on ....
9 get in ....
10 keep off ....

6 Report what you have written to the class. Say things like:

You put on your clothes.
You put up an umbrella.

Unit 38   Linking words together: Vowel + Consonant

Unit 38 practises linking words that end in a *vowel sound* with a word that begins with a *consonant sound*.

1 Repeat these phrases. Make sure you link the vowel sound at the end of the first word with the consonant sound at the beginning of the next.

1 a) foggy days   b) windy days

2 a) forty pounds   b) forty dollars

3 a) yellow carpets   b) blue carpets

4 a) primary school   b) secondary school

5 a) summer holidays   b) winter holidays

6 a) Friday night   b) Monday morning

2 Work with a partner. Discuss which of each pair (1(a) or 1(b); 2(a) or 2(b), etc.) you prefer or you would rather have. Some of these phrases might help you.

   I'd rather have … because …

   I think I prefer …

   … is/are better than … because …

   I like … but I don't like … . That's because …

Don't forget to link the final vowel to the initial consonant when you use the phrases in **1**. (And remember to link any final consonant + initial vowels, too.)

3 Work in pairs. Match the words in box A. One is done for you. Then listen and repeat. Make sure you link the consonant sounds at the ends of the words on the left with the vowel sounds at the start of the words on the right. 🔑

4 Match the words in box B in the same way. Then listen and repeat. Make sure you link the vowel sounds at the ends of the words on the left with the consonant sounds at the start of the words on the right. 🔑

A

post	•	•	agent
customs	•	•	office
head	•	•	assistant
smoke	•	•	alarm
travel	•	•	instrument
shop	•	•	officer
North	•	•	ache
musical	•	•	Africa

B

sore	•	•	shop
power	•	•	bike
Sahara	•	•	director
flower	•	•	box
company	•	•	station
computer	•	•	throat
motor	•	•	Desert
letter	•	•	keyboard

5 Work in pairs. Make connections between the phrases you have made in boxes A and B, and report your answers to the class. For example:

A post office and a power station are both buildings.

The Sahara Desert is in North Africa.

A flower shop may have several shop assistants.

Unit 39 Linking words together: Consonant + Consonant

1 Listen to these sentences. What is the second word in each sentence? Write it in the space. **O⟲**

1 We .... meet him again.
2 Please .... my shoes for me.
3 I .... bad after the party.
4 It .... before we got back.
5 I .... Peter to come.
6 We .... more milk.
7 This .... blanket isn't warm enough.
8 The .... problem's difficult.
9 I'll .... painting the house tomorrow.

2 Listen. If you compare the words said on their own with the words used in the sentences, you will hear that the *last consonant* of each word is pronounced differently. This often happens in connected speech, particularly when the consonants /t/, /d/ and /n / are followed by the sounds /m/, /b/ and /p/.

◄◄ 3 Listen again. Repeat each word you have written in **1** on its own and then repeat the whole sentence.

4 Repeat these phrases. Notice the change in the pronunciation of the consonant at the end of the first word.

1 last Monday	6 red bicycle	11 television programme
2 quite boring	7 old man	12 ten pounds
3 went back	8 around Britain	13 brown bag
4 met Bob	9 dead bird	14 seven million
5 most people	10 loud bang	15 broken mirror

5 Work in pairs. Write two sentences that include two or more of these phrases. For example:

<u>Last Monday</u> I watched a <u>television programme</u> on computers, but it was <u>quite boring</u>.

....

....

....

Unit 40   Sounds that link words: /w/ and /j/ ('y')

1 You will hear a conversation between Alan and Sue. Listen to the conversation and answer these questions.   🔑

1 When is Phil's birthday?

....

2 What present do Alan and Sue decide to buy for him?

....

3 When will they have a party?

....

2 Some of the words in the conversation are joined by a /w/ sound. Listen.

How‿about …   … throw‿it away.
   w   w

Some other words are joined by a /j/ ('y') sound. Listen.

… free‿on Saturday.   … Thursday‿evening.
     y   y

3 Repeat these sentences. The words marked are joined by a /w/ sound.

1 Do you know‿it's Phil's birthday?
                  w

2 What about a new‿umbrella?
                    w

3 That old blue‿one.
             w

4 Throw‿it away.
      w

5 Too‿expensive.
    w

6 How‿about Thursday?
    w

7 He's got an interview‿on Friday.
                    w

8 You‿arrange the party.
   w

4 Repeat these sentences. The words marked are joined by a /j/ ('y') sound.

1 It's Phil's birthday on Thursday.

2 We really ought to.

3 If we pay about £10 …

4 Thursday evening.

5 … free on Saturday.

5 Look at these sentences. Will the words marked be joined by /w/ or /j/ ('y')? One is done for you.

1 Who are you?

2 Germany imports gold.

3 Don't argue about it.

4 Coffee or tea?

5 I've been to Amsterdam.

6 Tomorrow afternoon.

7 Go away!

8 Hello, Ann!

9 Goodbye, Ann.

10 They weigh about five kilos.

6 Listen and repeat. Check your answers. 0—π

Unit 41 Sounds that link words: /r/

When a word that ends in the letter 'r' or in 're' is followed by a word that begins with a vowel sound, the words are usually linked with a /r/ sound.

1 Listen and repeat. First say the words on the left and then the phrase on the right.

1 for   for example

2 after   after all

3 further   further on

4 never   never again

5 your   your own

6 where   where are you

7 four   four o'clock

8 somewhere somewhere else

2 Repeat the words on the left.

door   1 Is the .... open?
hour   2 They've forgotten .... air tickets.
their   3 She's my .... -in-law.
neither   4 He started his new job a .... ago.
year   5 I've been waiting for an .... and a half.
mother   6 My .... is older than me.
far   7 Do you live .... away?
brother   8 .... am I.

3 Write the words in the sentences on the right. Repeat the sentences. Link the consonant sound at the end of the word with the vowel sound at the beginning of the next word. For example: 0—π

Is the door open?

4 Work in pairs. Match pairs of words in the box below. Two are done for you. 🔑

> October   mother⟵ under   summer   before   after
>
> winter   over   November   near ⟍ brother   far   here
>
> sooner   car ⟷ helicopter   beer   there ⟶ father   water
>
> sister   later

5 Report your pairs to the class. Say, for example:

  mother and father   car and helicopter
         r   r

Make sure you link the words with /r/.

Unit 42 Short sounds and sounds that are missed out

1 In connected speech the first, unstressed syllable of words that begin with the sound /ə/ is often very short and may be difficult to hear. For example:

  alive – He's alive.   along – It's along here.

2 Listen to these conversations and write the words you hear in the spaces. Use the context to help you. 🔑

  1 A: Where did Susan go?
     B: Just .... the road.

  2 A: Do you think I'm right?
     B: Yes, I .... completely.

  3 A: What time do we get to New York?
     B: Well, we should .... at six.

  4 A: Can't you sleep?
     B: No, I've been .... for hours.

  5 A: I didn't know Jim was in France.
     B: He's lived .... for three or four years now.

  6 A: Can you come out tonight?
     B: I'm .... I can't.

  7 A: Don't you get lonely in that big house?
     B: No, I like living ....

  8 A: Is the bank near here?
     B: Yes. It's .... five minutes ....

3 The 'h' sound at the beginning of some words is very short or may not be pronounced at all. Listen to these examples:

He likes it.   Does he like it?

4 Listen to these short conversations. 'h' sounds at the beginnings of words are marked. Draw a line through them if they are very short or not pronounced. Conversation 1 is done for you. 0⊸

1 A: Is that him over there?
   B: Who?
   A: The man who took your handbag?

2 A: He wasn't at home.
   B: No, I think he's on holiday.

3 A: How's Tom these days?
   B: Didn't you hear about his heart attack?

4 A: It says here, the Queen's coming.
   B: Where?
   A: Here.
   B: I do hope we'll be able to see her.

5 A: What are you children fighting about?
   B: It's MY book.
   A: HIS book's over there.
   B: HER book's over there. This one's mine!

5 Find the words that are sometimes pronounced with an 'h' sound and sometimes without. When *is* 'h' pronounced in these words? 0⊸

6 Work in pairs and say the conversations together.

Part 6 Intonation

<hr/>

Unit 43 Prominent words

1 Listen to these sentences. You will hear that one word is PROMINENT, or STANDS OUT from the rest. This is usually the word that the speaker sees as the most important in the sentence. Listen and circle the prominent word in each sentence. The first one is done for you.

1 (Thank) you.

2 I'm tired.

3 Chris did.

4 It's getting late.

5 I'm sure she will.

6 It's a lovely place.

7 She's in the sitting room.

8 It's raining again.

9 He's a postman.

10 We had a great time.

2 Listen again and repeat the sentences.

3 Match the answers in **1** with these sentences. One is done for you.

a) Who cooked dinner?   3....
b) This is for you.   ....
c) How was the holiday?   ....
d) What's the weather like?   ....
e) Do you like Wales?   ....

f) What does Dan do?   ....
g) You don't look very well.   ....
h) What time is it?   ....
i) Where's Suzie?   ....
j) Do you think she'll like it?   ....

4 Work in pairs and practise short conversations using the sentences in **1** and **3**.

<hr/>

Giving more details

5 Match words in A with words in B. How many things can you find that you might eat in a restaurant? Decide if they are a starter (S), main course (M) or dessert (D). Two are done for you.

A

chicken	tomato
cheese	cherry
apple	

B

| pie | salad |
| omelette | soup |

chicken salad (M)   tomato soup (S)

6 Repeat the names of some of the dishes. Make both words prominent.

7   In this exercise prominent words are written in CAPITAL LETTERS. Listen and repeat the sentences shown in the pictures. Notice that the repeated word is not prominent. This often happens to repeated words.

WHAT will you have for a STARTER?

I THINK I'll have some SOUP. TOMATO soup.

And for your MAIN course?

I'd LIKE a SALAD. CHICKEN salad.

And HOW about a DESSERT?

I'll HAVE some PIE, please. CHERRY pie.

8   Listen to this conversation and then work in pairs to make similar conversations.

Unit 44   Repeated words and prominence

1   Listen to these conversations. The prominent words are written in capital letters. Notice what happens to the word that is repeated.

1   A: She LOOKS a bit TIRED, DOESN'T she?
    B: YES. VERY tired.
2   A: Are you FREE on SUNDAY?
    B: What TIME on Sunday?

Listen again and repeat what B says. Now continue in the same way.

3   A: Have you got any in dark blue?   B: No, only light blue, I'm afraid.
4   A: Are you feeling better?   B: Oh, yes. Much better.
5   A: Shall we meet at one?   B: Can we make it half past one?
6   A: And the winning number is 5-4-9.   B: That's my number.
7   A: He's an artist, isn't he?   B: Yes, a very good artist, actually.
8   A: Did you say Tom was in the   B: No, the back garden.
       front garden?

2   Work in groups of three. One should take A's part, one B's part, and the third student should MONITOR what B says. Check particularly that the repeated word is not made prominent.

3 Listen. Which of the pictures below (a, b or c) is being described?

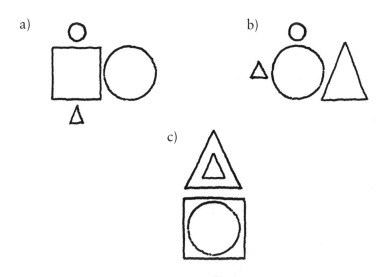

a)

b)

c)

4 Listen again to these sentences. Underline the words in the boxes that are prominent.

In the middle   is a big circle.
Above it   is a small circle.

On the left of the big circle   is a small triangle.
On the right   is a big triangle.

What do you notice about the repeated words?

5 Take a piece of paper and draw a picture similar to those in **3**. It should be made up of big and small circles, squares and triangles, and include four or five shapes in total. Don't let your partner see what you have drawn.

Then describe the picture to your partner. Your partner will try to draw what you describe on a separate piece of paper. When you have finished, compare your picture and your partner's drawing. Discuss any differences. Then repeat with your partner describing his or her picture to you.

Here are some words to help you:

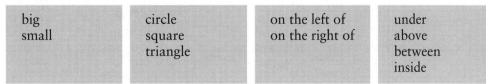

| big small | circle square triangle | on the left of on the right of | under above between inside |

Unit 45 More on prominent and non-prominent words

1 Complete the conversations with words from the box.

us	them	there	one	him	her	he

1 A: Do you want some grapes?
   B: No, thanks, I don't like ....

2 A: Wasn't that Peter?
   B: Sorry, I didn't see ....

3 A: Does Pat know the answer?
   B: I'll ask ....

4 A: What do you think of Scotland?
   B: I've never been ....

5 A: My son's called David.
   B: How old is ....?
   A: Three.

6 A: Does she live in this road?
   B: No, it's the next ....

7 A: I'm living in London now.
   B: Do you like it ....?

8 A: Can I book a table for tonight, please?
   B: Certainly. How many is it for?
   A: There'll be three of ....

2 Listen to the conversations and check your answers. Notice that the words you have written are not prominent. Why do you think this is? 🔑

3 Work in pairs. Say the conversations. Make sure that the words you have written are not prominent.

4 Complete the following with words from the box. 🔑

bottle	bunch	box
carton	packet	
tin	loaf	jar

1 A .... of cornflakes.
2 A .... of grapes.
3 A .... of jam.
4 A .... of bread.
5 A .... of beans.

6 A .... of lemonade.
7 A .... of coffee.
8 A .... of washing powder.
9 A .... of bananas.
10 A .... of yogurt.

5 Listen to this conversation. David is asking Ann to buy some things from the supermarket. Prominent words are in capital letters.

David: Can you get some CORNFLAKES?
Ann:　 Do you want a LARGE or SMALL packet?
David: A SMALL one.

6 Listen again and repeat the conversation a line at a time. Notice that words are prominent where there is a CHOICE.

Can you get some ⟨CORNFLAKES?⟩　　Cornflakes, not
　　　　　　　　　　　　　　　　　　coffee or yogurt, etc.

Do you want a ⟨LARGE⟩ or ⟨SMALL⟩ packet?

A ⟨SMALL⟩ one.　　　　　　　　　　　　　Not prominent
　　　　　　　　　　　　　　　　　　　　because there is
　　　　　　　　　　　　　　　　　　　　no choice – you
Small, not　　Large, not　　Small, not　　normally buy
large　　　　small　　　　　large　　　　cornflakes in a
　　　　　　　　　　　　　　　　　　　　packet

7 Work in pairs and make conversations using the same pattern.

Can you get some .... ?

Do you want a large or small .... ?

A .... one.

Unit 46   Falling and rising tones

1   Listen to these examples. Prominent words are in capital letters. Notice how the voice FALLS at the end.

It's MINE.   She's from ROME.   Is it YOURS?

I MET him at a DISCO.

Now listen to these examples. Notice how the voice RISES at the end.

I THINK so.   PROBABLY.   Are they HERE yet?

Is THIS the PARIS train?

2   Listen to these sentence halves. Write (↘) in the space if the voice falls at the end and write (↗) if it goes up. Two are done for you.

1	a) I went to London … (↘)	b)	… on Saturday. (↗)
2	a) David … ( )	b)	… works in a bookshop. ( )
3	a) There's some cake … ( )	b)	… in the kitchen. ( )
4	a) In Hong Kong … ( )	b)	… last year. ( )
5	a) I'm fairly sure … ( )	b)	… it's upstairs. ( )
6	a) Yes, … ( )	b)	… of course. ( )
7	a) Turn left here … ( )	b)	… then go straight on. ( )
8	a) Oh dear, … ( )	b)	… I *am* sorry. ( )
9	a) I like it … ( )	b)	… very much. ( )
10	a) I don't smoke … ( )	b)	… thank you. ( )

3   Listen again. Repeat the sentence halves and check your answers. ⚷

4   Repeat the two halves of the sentence together. For example, say:

I went to London on Saturday.

5   Work in pairs. Match the answers in **2** with these sentences. One is done for you. ⚷

a) What does your son do now?   2....   f) Would you like one?   ....
b) I'm hungry.   ....   g) How do I get to the station?   ....
c) How was the weekend?   ....   h) Can I sit here?   ....
d) What do you think of the   ....   i) Where did you buy that radio?   ....
   food here?   j) I'm afraid I can't come with you. ....
e) Where did I leave my briefcase? ....

6   Work in pairs. Practise short conversations using the sentences in **2** and **5**.

7   It is Saturday and Mandy and Paul are talking about what they should do. Listen. Prominent words are in capital letters and the arrows show how the voice falls or rises.

Notice how Paul uses a RISING tone (◀) for the subject they are already talking about and a FALLING tone (◥) to give new information.

8   Listen again and repeat the conversations a line at a time.

9   Work in pairs. Make similar conversations using the same intonation. These notes will help you.

1 … visit your sister	… saw Mary … Tuesday
2 … go for a walk	… went to the park … Wednesday
3 … watch TV	… stayed at home … Thursday
4 …. go to the theatre	… saw a play … yesterday

Unit 47   Reasons for falling and rising

Remember that a falling tone gives some new information and a rising tone is used for a subject that is already being talked about.

1   Would you expect the tone in each part of B's sentences to fall or to rise? Write ◥ or ◀ in the spaces. Study these examples first.

1   A: My brother is an accountant. He builds bridges.
     B: But engineers (◥) build bridges (◀).

B repeats 'build bridges' so we would expect that part to have a rising tone. The 'engineers' part is new information, so we would expect that part to have a falling tone.

2   A: What shall we do after lunch?
     B: After we've eaten (◀) we could go and see Kate (◥).

'After we've eaten' here means the same as 'after lunch', so we would expect it to have a rising tone. The suggestion about visiting Kate is new information, so we would expect it to have a falling tone.

Now work in pairs and talk about these in the same way.

3　A: When are you going to New York?
　　B: I'm flying (　) at ten o'clock (　).

4　A: When did you first meet Tony?
　　B: I've known him (　) for years (　).

5　A: How long have you been able to speak French?
　　B: I've been learning French (　) for six years (　).

6　A: When did you last see Mike?
　　B: Tuesday (　) was the last time I saw him (　).

7　A: Do I turn it on with this switch?
　　B: Press the red one (　) not the black one (　).

8　A: Have you seen the papers I brought home?
　　B: Your papers (　) are on the table (　) in the kitchen (　).

2　Listen and check your answers. Then work in pairs. Take A and B's parts and say the conversations together.　○─╦

3　Think of an answer to the following questions.

'What's your favourite …?'

colour	drink	car	food
time of the year		town	country

4　Listen to this conversation.　○─╦

A: WHAT'S your FAVOURITE COLOUR?

B: RED. WHAT'S YOURS?

A: MY favourite's BLUE.

Notice the tones in 'RED' and 'MY favourite's BLUE'. Why do you think these tones are used?

Now work in pairs and make conversations about the things in **3**. Use this pattern.

A: WHAT'S your FAVOURITE ....?

B: .... WHAT'S YOURS?

A: MY favourite's ....

Unit 48　A second rising tone

In Units 46 and 47, you learnt to hear the difference between a rising tone and a falling tone and to understand what each means. There is another common tone in English which first falls and then rises. It has many of the same uses as the rising tone.

1　Listen to these short sentences and decide if the tone at the end is: ⚷

a) FALLING ◣　　b) RISING ◤　　c) FALLING-RISING ＼◤

The first three are done for you. Notice that the tone starts in the last prominent word.

1　CAN you?	..*b*..	6	What TIME is it?	....
2　That's FINE.	..*a*..	7	It's BEAUTIFUL.	....
3　PROBABLY.	..*c*..	8	SOMETIMES.	....
4　You DIDN'T!	....	9	I HOPE so.	....
5　Is THIS right?	....	10	HAVE another BISCUIT.	....

2　Listen to these short conversations. Concentrate particularly on what B says in each. The prominent words in B's parts are in capital letters. The first tone B uses is shown with an arrow. Is the second tone B uses the same or different? Write S or D in the space. ⚷

		Same (S) or Different (D)?
1 A:Shall we go for a drive?	B: YES ◣ – I'd LOVE to. ◣	S
2 A:Have you finished painting?	B: NO ◣ – NOT YET.	
3 A:Can you come on Monday?	B: YES ◣ – I THINK so.	
4 A:Do you mind if I smoke?	B: NO ◣ – not REALLY.	
5 A:Bye.	B: BYE ◤ – see you TOMORROW.	
6 A:Are you going on holiday this year?	B: PERHAPS ＼◤ – I don't KNOW yet.	
7 A:Jim and Sheila are getting married!	B: REALLY ＼◤ – I THOUGHT they would.	
8 A:When are you going to London?	B: on SUNDAY ◣ – IF the WEATHER'S good.	

3　Listen again and decide what the second tone is that B uses in each sentence. Draw arrows to show if the tone is falling, rising or falling-rising. For example: ⚷

1 B: YES ◣ – I'd LOVE to. ◣

4　Work in pairs. Take A and B's parts and say the short conversations together. A should check that B is using the correct tones.

────────── **Correcting something that has been said**

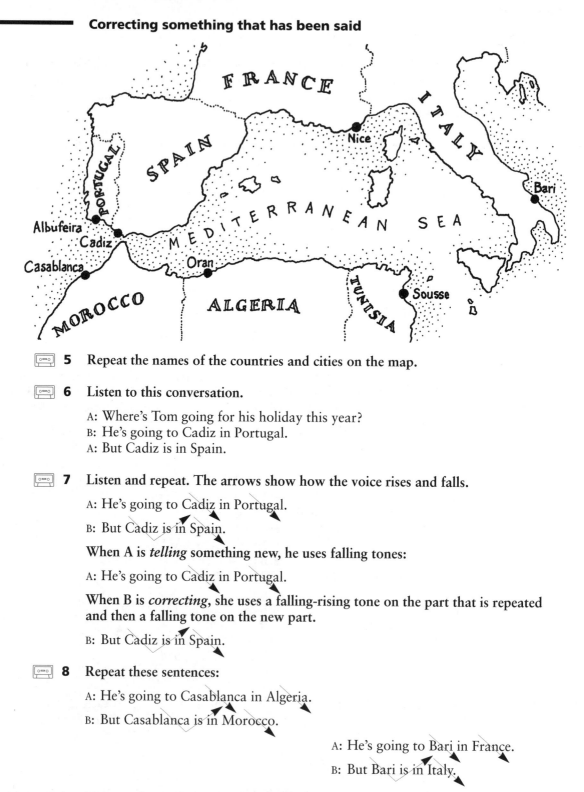

5　Repeat the names of the countries and cities on the map.

6　Listen to this conversation.

A: Where's Tom going for his holiday this year?
B: He's going to Cadiz in Portugal.
A: But Cadiz is in Spain.

7　Listen and repeat. The arrows show how the voice rises and falls.

A: He's going to Cadiz in Portugal.

B: But Cadiz is in Spain.

When A is *telling* something new, he uses falling tones:

A: He's going to Cadiz in Portugal.

When B is *correcting*, she uses a falling-rising tone on the part that is repeated and then a falling tone on the new part.

B: But Cadiz is in Spain.

8　Repeat these sentences:

A: He's going to Casablanca in Algeria.

B: But Casablanca is in Morocco.

A: He's going to Bari in France.

B: But Bari is in Italy.

9　Now work in pairs and make similar conversations.

Unit 49 Tonic words

1 The word in a sentence on which the fall or rise (or fall-rise) begins is called the TONIC WORD. Listen to these examples.

MY name's PETER.   HAVE you BEEN there?   I USED to play.

2 Listen to these sentences and circle the tonic word in each. The first one is done for you.

a) It's on (top) of the bookcase.   d) At five past one.

b) With milk, please.   e) It's on top of the bookcase.

c) At five past one.   f) With milk, please.

3 Listen again. Repeat the sentences and check your answers.

4 Work in pairs and decide which of the sentences in **2** best follows these sentences. The first one is done for you.

1 A: Did you want tea without milk?   B: *f.....*
2 A: See you at ten past one.   B: ....
3 A: Where's the newspaper?   B: ....
4 A: Did you want tea with lemon?   B: ....
5 A: I thought I put the newspaper on the bookcase. B: ....
6 A: See you at five to one.   B: ....

5 Listen to the recording and check your answers. Then work in pairs and say the short conversations together.

6 Look at these conversations. Which do you think will be the TONIC WORD in the missing sentences? Complete the conversations as in the first example, writing the tonic word in each in capital letters.

1 A: Can I HELP you?
   B: *I'm looking for a DRESS.....*
      (I'm looking for a dress.)
   A: They're on the SECOND floor.
   B: *THANK you.....*
      (Thank you.)

2 A: What do you THINK?
   B: ....
      (I don't like the colour.)
   A: I thought you LIKED red.
   B: ....
      (I prefer blue.)

3 A: Shall we eat HERE?

B: ....
(Let's sit over there.)

A: Under THAT tree?

B: ....
(The other one.)

7 Listen and check your answers. 🔑

◀◀ **8** Listen again. Repeat the conversations a line at a time. Then work in pairs and say the conversations together.

Unit 50 Predicting tones

1 In some of the lines of these conversations, the TONE is shown. Predict what it is going to be in the other lines. Draw arrows starting at the TONIC WORD.

1 A: Was it EXPENSIVE?

B: QUITE expensive.

A: How MUCH?

B: A thousand POUNDS.

2 A: Is it still RAINING?

B: I THINK so.

A: HEAVILY?

B: Not VERY.

3 A: What's on TV tonight?

B: A HORROR film.

A: Is it GOOD?

B: I've HEARD it is.

2 Listen and check your answers. 🔑

◄◄ ▭ **3**   Listen again. Repeat the conversations a line at a time. Then work in pairs and say the conversations together.

▭ **4**   Repeat these sentences with the intonation shown.

1   I ALWAYS have lunch there.

2   Shall we go TONIGHT?

3   She plays TENNIS every WEEK.

4   I'd LIKE to.

5   I'd LIKE to.

Now work in pairs and write five short conversations each of which includes one of these sentences with the intonation shown. An example is done for you. Then perform your conversations for the rest of the class.

1   A: *Shall we have lunch?*
      B: *OK. Let's go to the snack bar.*
      A: *Why there?*
      B: *I ALWAYS have lunch there.*

Part 7 Sounds and grammar

Unit 51 Weak and strong forms; short and long forms

1 Many common grammar words in English have a STRONG form and a WEAK form.
Listen. You will hear the STRONG forms of these words:

does	but	from

Now listen again. You will hear short sentences with the WEAK forms of the same words.

Does she play golf?
I need a new car, but I haven't got any money.
It's a letter from Steve.

Repeat the sentences. All the WEAK forms of the words you will practise in Part 7 contain the sound /ə/.

Weak and strong forms: three verbs with weak forms: *do*, *does* and *can*

2 Repeat these questions. Pronounce the verbs *do*, *does* and *can* with their weak forms.

1 Do you like it? 4 Can I take two? 7 Why does she want to leave?
2 Can we go now? 5 Does it hurt? 8 Where can we see one?
3 Does he live here? 6 When do you go back? 9 How do you feel now?

3 Work in pairs. Match each question from **2** with one of the answers below. One is done for you. Then say the short conversations together.

3.... No, next door.   .... In a zoo.   .... Yes, of course.
.... A bit later.   .... Much better.   .... Tomorrow.
.... She's tired.   .... Not really.   .... Yes, very much.

Short and long forms

4 The negative forms of the same verbs have a SHORT form and a LONG form. They are written like this:

SHORT FORM	don't	doesn't	can't
LONG FORM	do not	does not	can not (*or* cannot)

The short form is normally used in speaking and is sometimes used in writing, particularly writing in an informal style.

5 Work in pairs. Ask your partner the questions below. Use the *weak* forms of the verbs. Write a tick (✓) or a cross (✗) in the spaces.

Answer using short forms like this:

| Yes, I do. | No, I don't. |
| Yes, I can. | No, I can't. |

Do you like cheese?   ....
Can you speak Italian?   ....
Do you live in a flat?   ....
Can you play football well?   ....
Do you smoke?   ....
Can you type well?   ....
Do you know any famous people?   ....
Can you swim?   ....

6 Report back to the class only the NEGATIVE answers like this:

Do you like cheese?   ✗....   Maria doesn't like cheese.

Can you speak Italian?   ✓....   –

Do you live in a flat?   ✓....   –

Can you play football well? ✗....   Maria can't play football well.

Unit 52 Long and short forms of verbs

1 In this unit you will practise some more verbs that have a LONG form and a SHORT form in spoken English.

LONG FORM WRITTEN AS:	SHORT FORM WRITTEN AS:	LONG FORM WRITTEN AS:	SHORT FORM WRITTEN AS:
would	'd	is	's
should	'd	are	're
had	'd	has	's
will	'll	have	've
shall	'll	am	'm

2 Listen to this conversation. Write what you hear in the spaces. 🔑

A: .... like some of those apples, please. How much ....?

B: .... twelve pence each. How many .... like?

A: .... have five, please.

B: There you are. .... put them in a bag for you?

A: Oh, ...? .... very kind of you.

B: Anything else?

A: No, ... all thanks. How much ....?

B: .... be 60 pence, please.

A: .... a £5 note.

B: .... got anything smaller?

A: Er ... oh, yes. .... got a pound coin.

◄◄ **3** Listen again and repeat the conversation a sentence at a time. Then work in pairs and say the conversation together. Don't forget to use SHORT forms where you have written them.

4 From the examples in this conversation try to complete this sentence. It will give a simple rule to help you decide when to use the LONG form. 🔑

The LONG form of these verbs is used in ....

5 Look at this family and listen to the description.

Judy's 34 and Adrian's 35.
They've been married for five years.
They've got two children.
Pat's three and David's two.

Now describe these families in the same way. Make sure you use the short forms of the verbs.

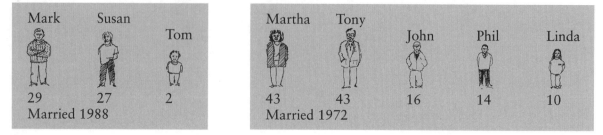

6 Work in pairs. Make WRONG sentences about the families. Listen to these examples.

A: Mark's 28.
B: No, he's not. He's 29.

A: Martha and Tony've been married for 18 years.
B: No, they haven't. They've been married for 21 years.

A: Adrian and Judy've got three children.
B: No, they haven't. They've got two children.

Now continue in the same way. Use the short form of the verbs.

7 Look back at the sentences in **5**. If you have a friend, brother or sister who has a family, tell your partner about the family in the same way.

Unit 53 More on the long and short forms of verbs

1 Work in pairs. Match the questions on the left with the answers on the right. One is done for you.

How old are you?   •   • I'll go tomorrow.
Is she here?   •   • Yes, I've been twice.
When will you go?   •   • I'm twenty-one.
Shall we eat now?   •   • No, she's in town.
Have you been before?   •   • I'd rather wait until later.

Now repeat the conversations a line at a time and check your answers. Use the long form of the verbs in the questions and the short form in the answers. O→

2 Work in pairs and say the conversations together.

3 Do the same for these questions and answers – match the questions and answers, repeat them and check your answers, and then say the conversations in pairs. O→

What's your name?   •   • I'm sorry. The train was late.
When're they going?   •   • They've got to be home by 11.
What's Jim got?   •   • I'm making dinner.
Where've you been?   •   • It's Rachel Jones.
What're you doing?   •   • It's a present.

Notice that in these questions the verbs 'is', 'are', 'has' and 'have' have their short forms. These verbs usually have their short forms even in questions.

4 Mrs Jones has two children. They went to play in the park but should have been home an hour ago. She is very worried and phones the police. Listen to part of the conversation and decide which of these pictures shows Tom and which shows Paul. ⚷

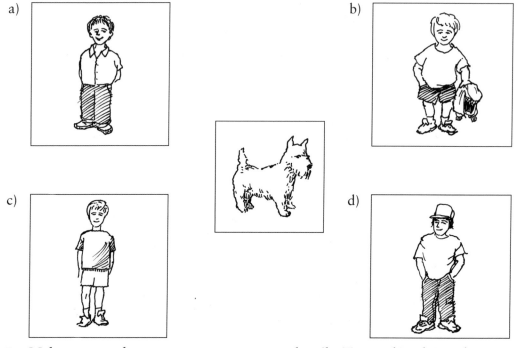

a)

b)

c)

d)

5 Make as many short sentences as you can to describe Tom and Paul. Use the pictures to help you.

6 Work in pairs. Choose another student in your class and describe him or her in the same way. Your partner should try to guess who you are describing.

Unit 54 Weak and strong forms of some conjunctions

1 Which of these three words in the box do you hear in these sentences? Write one word in each space.

and	or	but

1 a) Milk .... no sugar.
  b) Milk .... no sugar.
2 a) Paul .... Alison.
  b) Paul .... Alison.
3 a) It was small .... very heavy.
  b) It was small .... very heavy.

4 a) Jean .... her friend.
  b) Jean .... her friend.
5 a) .... I want to go.
  b) .... I want to go.
6 a) Red .... green.
  b) Red .... green.

◄◄ 🔲 **2** Listen again. Repeat the sentences and check your answers. Notice that the words are pronounced with their WEAK form. 🔑

3 Work in pairs. Say a sentence from **1**. Your partner should decide which of the sentences you are saying and should answer '1(b)', '2(a)', etc. Make sure you use the short form of the word in each case.

🔲 **4** Here are two more words with a weak and a strong form. 🔑

> as   than

Look at the information in the map below. Listen to these sentences and try to decide if they are true (T) or false (F). Notice that the weak forms of 'as' and 'than' are always used.

1 .... 2 .... 3 .... 4 .... 5 .... 6 .... 7 .... 8 ....

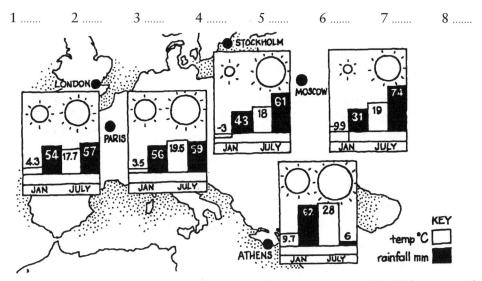

5 Work in pairs. Make sentences about the information. Some should be true and some false. Your partner should decide if they are true or false. Here is some language to help you. (Remember to use the weak forms of 'as' and 'than'.)

In January	Paris	is	wetter	than	Athens.
July	Stockholm		hotter		Moscow.
	London		colder		
			sunnier		
			drier		

In January	Paris	is (about)	hot		Athens.
July	Stockholm		as cold	as	Moscow.
	London		sunny		
			the same temperature		

Unit 55   Weak and strong forms of some prepositions

1   Look at these sentences. Decide which of these prepositions can fit into each space: **O—π**

at	for	from	of	to

Write your answers in the spaces on the right. One is done for you.

1 He was looking .... the children in the park.   *for* ...... / *at* ......
2 I was at home .... six o'clock.   .... / ....
3 They drove .... Glasgow last night.   .... / ....
4 He had a drawing .... Rome.   .... / ....
5 She picked up the ball and threw it .... her brother.   .... / ....
6 Do you like this picture? It's a present .... Sue.   .... / ....
7 The people .... France drink a lot of wine.   .... / ....
8 She pointed .... the ship.   .... / ....

2   Now listen to the sentences and write the word you hear in the spaces in the sentences. **O—π**

3   Look at this table. Notice that all these prepositions have at least two pronunciations – a STRONG FORM and a WEAK FORM. Listen and repeat the prepositions. First repeat the STRONG FORM and then the WEAK FORM.

	STRONG FORM	WEAK FORM
at	/æt/	/ət/
for	/fɔː/	/fə/
from	/frɒm/	/frəm/
of	/ɒv/	/əv/
to	/tuː/	/tə/

4   Now repeat the sentences from **1**. They are recorded again on the tape. Use the WEAK forms of the prepositions.

5   Listen to these sentences. Write S in the spaces if you hear the STRONG form of the preposition and W if you hear the WEAK form. **O—π**

1 What are you looking at?   ....   6 These flowers are for you.   ....
2 He wants to visit Canada.   ....   7 It's not to Bill, it's from Bill.   ....
3 Is it made of plastic?   ....   8 What's it made of?   ....
4 Where did you get it from?   ....   9 Shall we meet at three?   ....
5 What do you want it for?   ....   10 But I want to.   ....

6   Listen again and repeat the sentences. Try to decide when the STRONG forms of the prepositions are used. **O—π**

7 Listen to this person talking about her plans for a driving holiday around England. Follow the route she plans to take on the map.

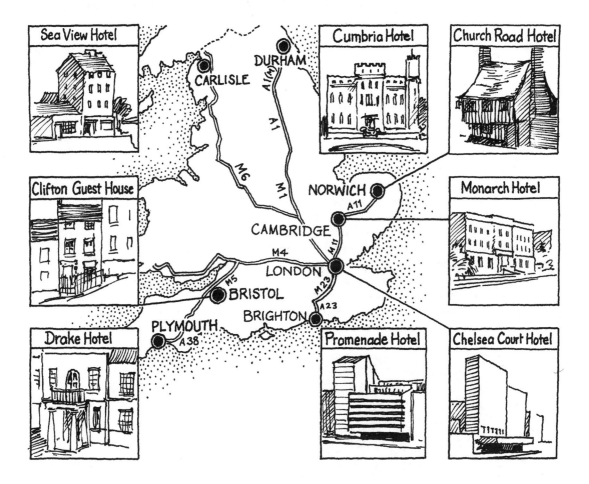

8 Plan *your* holiday using the same map and then tell your partner about it. You would like to see as much of the country as possible, but you only have 10 days. You need to plan your holiday carefully – the route, where you are going to stay, and how long in each place. Remember to use the 'going to' future tense and the weak forms of the prepositions 'at', 'for', 'from', 'of' and 'to'.

Unit 56 The pronunciation of '-ed' endings

1 Last week Jane Bradbury saw an accident from her office window. Later she told a friend about what she had seen. As you listen, decide which of these headlines appeared in the local newspaper the following day. 🔑

Man knocked down by speeding motorbike

Man injured by ambulance

Man and woman killed crossing road

Man injured by car on crossing

◄◄ ▱ **2**   Listen to the story again, and then try to retell the story. Some of the sentences below and the words in the box may help you. The missing words are all past tense '-ed' words.

Jane Bradbury was working in her office.
She .... to see what the weather was like.
She .... to the window and .... outside.
A car .... at the crossing.
A man and a woman .... to cross the road.
Another car drove over the crossing.
The woman .... out of the way.
The car .... her.
It .... down the man.
Jane .... for an ambulance and the police.
They .... quickly.
The ambulance men .... the woman to stand up.
They .... the man into the ambulance.
Jane .... what she had seen.
Later, the police .... the driver.

walked	stopped
knocked	phoned
jumped	arrived
wanted	started
looked	helped
explained	carried
arrested	missed

▱ **3**   Repeat the words in the box in **2**.

◄◄ ▱ **4**   '-ed' endings are pronounced in one of three ways. Listen again to the past tense '-ed' words from the story and write them in this table according to the pronunciation of '-ed': ⊙⊼

/t/	/d/	/ɪd/

5 The pronunciation of '-ed' depends on the sound that comes before it. This table shows the letters that come before '-ed' in the verbs in **4** when it is pronounced these three ways:

/t/			/d/		/ɪd/
k	p	s	n	v	t

6 Have you ever seen an accident or been involved in one? Tell your partner or the class about it. Pay particular attention to the pronunciation of past tense '-ed' endings.

Unit 57   More on the pronunciation of '-ed' endings

1 Work in pairs. Choose words from the box to complete these conversations. All the words end in '-ed'. **0-**

laughed	walked	rained	arrived	finished	mended
dropped	washed	passed	polluted	posted	

1 A: How was the weather?
   B: It .... all the time.

2 A: How did your glass break?
   B: I .... it.

3 A: Why didn't you swim?
   B: The sea was ....

4 A: Your letter hasn't .... yet.
   B: But I .... it on Tuesday.

5 A: When can I see the painting?
   B: Not until I've .... it.

6 A: How did the driving test go?
   B: I ....!

7 A: Was the film funny?
   B: Yes, I .... all the time.

8 A: Is it still broken?
   B: No, I've .... it.

9 A: This floor is dirty.
   B: But I .... it yesterday.

10 A: You look tired.
   B: I've .... all the way.

2 Repeat the conversations a line at a time and check your answers. Then say them with your partner.

3 Using the '-ed' verbs in **1**, add letters to the table in task **4**, Unit 56. **0-**

4 Work in pairs. Tell a story to the rest of the class based on one of the pairs of pictures below. They show the beginning and end of the story. The first sentence is given for each. Make notes and try to include as many past tense verbs ending in '-ed' as you can. Some notes for the first set are given below as an example. The complete story is on the recording. ⊙‑

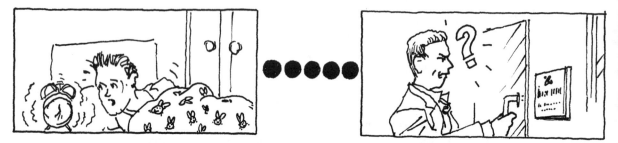

One day Tom woke up and <u>realised</u> that he was late for work.   ...

Tom woke up — realis<u>ed</u> late. Wash<u>ed</u>, shav<u>ed</u> & brush<u>ed</u> teeth. Hurri<u>ed</u> downstairs & walk<u>ed</u> to bus stop. Wait<u>ed</u> 5 minutes. Bus arriv<u>ed</u>. Got to office, discover<u>ed</u> closed. Forgotten it was Sunday!

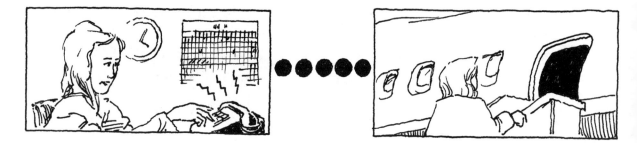

The phone rang and Jean <u>answered</u> it.   ...

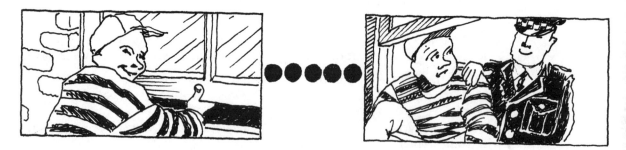

The burglar <u>opened</u> the window quietly.   ...

Unit 58   The pronunciation of '-s' endings

1 The '-s' at the end of words is pronounced either as /s/, /z/ or /ɪz/.
Repeat these example words:

1 These words end with /s/:   speaks, keeps, cats
2 These words end with /z/:   calls, comes, toys
3 These words end with /ɪz/:   catches, passes, boxes

The pronunciation used depends on the sound that comes before the final '-s'
or '-es'.

2 Listen to these groups of words. In each group all the words except one have the
same pronunciation at the end. Underline the odd one out in each group. ⚷

1 looks, sleeps, runs, cuts, hopes
2 finishes, includes, chooses, switches, washes
3 teaches, phones, gives, cleans, buys
4 plays, stays, rains, happens, gets
5 forgets, sits, speaks, touches, stops
6 begins, promises, drives, seems, sells

3 Listen again and repeat the words in each group. Decide which letters are
followed by the sounds /s/, /z/ and /ɪz/ and write them in the table. Some are
done for you. ⚷

/z/		/s/		/ɪz/
n	d	k	p	s

4 Work in pairs. Study these pictures for one minute. Then cover the pictures and
try to remember what you saw. Your partner will check your answers.
Concentrate on pronouncing the plural 's' correctly.

5   Look again at the things shown in the pictures in **4**. How is the plural 's' pronounced in each? If necessary, add more sounds to the table in **3**.   O⟋

6   Work in pairs. Decide what shop you would go to to buy these things: O⟋

cigarettes	shoes	matches	jeans	socks	sweets
gloves	biscuits	slippers	cornflakes	cakes	nails
potatoes					

Report your answers to the rest of the class. Concentrate on the correct pronunciation of the final '-s' or '-es'.

Part 8 Pronouncing written words

Unit 59   Letters and sounds

Written LETTERS stand for spoken SOUNDS. In some words each letter stands for one sound – for example, in the word 'fog' (/fɒg/). In other words there are more letters than sounds – for example, in the word 'luck' (/lʌk/).

1 Work in pairs. Decide if the number of letters and sounds in these words is the same (S) or different (D). The first two examples are done for you.

	S	D		S	D		S	D
fog	☑	☐	winter	☐	☐	not	☐	☐
luck	☐	☑	shut	☐	☐	thin	☐	☐
cough	☐	☐	chess	☐	☐	other	☐	☐
cut	☐	☐	bill	☐	☐	touch	☐	☐
plan	☐	☐	dust	☐	☐			

2 Repeat the words and check your answers. ⌐⊙

3 Study the words in the box below and decide how many ways the *consonant letters* can be pronounced. Write 1 in the box next to the consonant if it is pronounced in only one way and 2 if it is pronounced in two ways. ⌐⊙

keep	five	spin	want	ahead	moon	bite	age
kilo	red	cat	double	win	hat	after	police
gram	visa						

b ☐   f ☐   k ☐   n ☐   s ☐   w ☐
c ☐   g ☐   l ☐   p ☐   t ☐
d ☐   h ☐   m ☐   r ☐   v ☐

Most single consonant letters have only one pronunciation. What consonant letters have you found that have *two* common pronunciations?

4 Look at this 'word chain'.

example easy yes sugar rain no outside

The first letter of each word begins with the last letter of the previous word. Make word chains around the class.

If you give a wrong word or can't think of a new word you are out of the chain. Don't repeat a word in a chain.

Unit 60 Pronouncing consonant letters 'c' and 'g'

1 In columns 1 and 2 below, underline all the 'c's that are pronounced /s/, and circle all the 'c's that are pronounced /k/. The first line is done for you.

1		2
a) The traffic's bad ...	•	• ... America twice.
b) After the cinema, ...	•	• ... a parcel.
c) I've been to ...	•	• ... the police!
d) Only take this medicine ...	•	• ... in the city centre.
e) I went across the road ...	•	• ... in an emergency.
f) I had to collect ...	•	• ... since December.
g) I haven't had a cigarette ...	•	• ... we went to a disco.
h) Call ...	•	• ... to the post office.

2 Work in pairs. Match the sentence halves in columns 1 and 2.

3 Repeat the sentences and check your answers. ⊙⚿

4 Complete this rule to tell you when to pronounce the letter 'c' as /s/ (sit) and when as /k/ (cat). ⊙⚿

The letter 'c' is pronounced /s/ before the letters ...., ... or .... in a word, and pronounced /k/ everywhere else.

5 The rule for pronouncing the letter 'g' is similar to the rule for pronouncing 'c'. It is pronounced /dʒ/ (page) before the letters 'e', 'i' and 'y', and it is pronounced /g/ (gave) everywhere else. But there are some common exceptions to this rule. Underline the words in the box that break the rule. First try to do it without the recording, then repeat the words and check your answers. ⊙⚿

goodbye	together	grandparents	stranger	bag	girl	cigarette
dangerous	again	begin	Egypt	grass	give	engine
change	get	large	language	vegetables	Germany

6 Write one sentence which includes two or more words including the letter 'g'. Use the words in **5** or others you can think of. For example:

My grandparents went to Germany in August.

Show your sentence to other members of the class and ask them to read it aloud. Check that they pronounce 'g' correctly.

Unit 61 Pronouncing 'th'

1 The consonant pair 'th' can have two pronunciations, /θ/ (think) and /ð/ (these). The rule for pronouncing 'th' at the *beginning* of a word is that it is normally pronounced /θ/ (think) except in a few grammar words (the, they, them, their, this, that, these, those, than, then, there and though).

2 Match these questions and answers. One is done for you.

How many are there?　●　● Through here.
What's the matter?　●　● On Thursday.
Is this yours?　●　● I'm thirsty.
What time's their train?　●　● A thousand.
Where are they?　●　● No, he's thinner.
Is he fatter than me?　●　● At three twenty-five.
What day are you going there?　●　● Yes, thank you.

3 Listen and check your answers. When you have done this, listen again and repeat the conversations a line at a time. ०━〒

4 Work in pairs. Say these words to your partner, and then complete the rule. ०━〒

| mouth | birth | fourth | path |
| fifth | worth | month | north |

When 'th' is at the end of a word it is pronounced / /.

5 'th' comes in the middle of these words. Work in pairs and underline the words in which 'th' is pronounced /ð/. ०━〒

| father | bathroom | nothing | other | weather | birthday |
| something | together | authority | either | rather | healthy |

What do you notice about the ends of the words you have underlined? Complete this sentence to give you a simple rule about the pronunciation of 'th' in the middle of words.

'th' in the middle of a word is usually pronounced / / if the word ends in '........'.

6 Repeat the words in the boxes in **4** and **5**.

7 Work in pairs. Try to match the dates and the events. Then report back your decisions to the rest of the class. ⚿

Josef Stalin died

Mrs Thatcher became Prime Minister

The first football World Cup began in Uruguay

13th July 1930   5th March 1953   16th September 1963   8th April 1973   3rd May 1979   3rd July 1983

State of Malaysia was created

John McEnroe won Wimbledon

Pablo Picasso died

Unit 62 Pronouncing 'sh', 'ch' and 'gh'

1 Work in pairs. Study the words in the box and answer the questions below.

shoes	washing machine	night	shampoo	Chinese	tough
ship	high	toothbrush	cheese	rough	sharp	ghost
shiver	shop	fish	shirt	fresh	church	cough
laugh	British	dishwasher				

1 How many ways are there of pronouncing 'sh'? ....
2 'ch' is usually pronounced /tʃ/ (as in <u>ch</u>eese). Find one word where it is pronounced differently. ....
3 Find a word where 'gh' is pronounced /f/. ....
4 Find a word where 'gh' is not pronounced at all. ....
5 Find a word where 'gh' is pronounced in another way. ....

2 Repeat the words and check your answers. 〇ﾗ

3 Work in pairs. In the box in **1** find … 〇ﾗ

1 two things you can see in a bathroom .... & ....
2 two things you can eat .... & ....
3 two things you wear .... & ....
4 two things you can see in a kitchen .... & ....
5 two things you do when you are ill .... & ....
6 two buildings .... & ....
7 two things you can see at sea .... & ....
8 two words that can describe food .... & ....
9 two nationalities .... & ....
10 two words to describe how something
  feels when you touch it .... & ....

4 Report your answers to the class.

5 Work in pairs. Write sentences for A to make short conversations. Then say the conversations together for the rest of the class.

1 A: ....
  B: When I've finished washing up.
2 A: ....
  B: She wrote a cheque.
3 A: ....
  B: I hadn't got enough change.
4 A: ....
  B: I bought some shoes.
5 A: ....
  B: I didn't eat much for lunch.

Unit 63 Pronunciation, spelling and word stress

1 Look at these words. How are the underlined letters pronounced?

corn<u>er</u>   <u>a</u>cross   c<u>o</u>rrect   mag<u>a</u>zine   nons<u>e</u>nse

2 This sound is /ə/, sometimes called 'schwa'. It has many different spellings in English.
  Work in pairs. Circle the letter or letters that are pronounced /ə/ in these words. The first one is done for you.

daught(er)   camera   company   condition   petrol   neighbour
handsome   abroad   England   doctor   pronunciation

3 Repeat the words and check your answers. 〇ﾗ

4   Repeat the words in the box.

| supper | suppose | commercial | common | collect | collar |
| concert | continue | person | percent | | |

5   Work in pairs. In the words in the box in **4**: ⚷

a) <u>underline</u> the stressed syllable, and
b) circle any /ə/ sounds.

Then listen again and check your answers.

6   Complete these sentences with the words on the right: ⚷

/ə/ is the common pronunciation of
.... syllables. It is never the
vowel sound in .... syllables.

| stressed |
| unstressed |

7   Work in pairs. Look at this picture and find as many things as you can that have a /ə/ in their pronunciation. Write the words in the spaces and circle the /ə/ sounds. Two are done for you. ⚷

– mot(o)rbike...................
   cin(e)m(a)....................
   ....
   ....
   ....
   ....
   ....
   ....
   ....
   ....
   ....
   ....
   ....
   ....
   ....
   ....
   ....
   ....
   ....
   ....

How many ways have you found of spelling the /ə/ sound? Write them here. Two are done for you.

o,r,e,...

Unit 64   Pronouncing single vowel letters

In Unit 64 you will learn a rule for deciding how to pronounce the vowel in words of one syllable. The rule for pronouncing vowels in the stressed syllables of words made up of more than one syllable is complicated. The best thing to do is to try to learn the pronunciation and stress when you learn the word.

1   Repeat the NAMES of these vowel letters.

a   e   i   o   u

2   Work in pairs. Say these abbreviations. ⊶

U.S.A.   E.C.   P.T.O.   I.O.U.   U.N.   U.K.   U.A.E.   W.H.O.

What do they stand for?

3   Repeat the abbreviations in **2**.

4   All the words in the box below have one syllable with one vowel letter in the middle. Underline all the words that have a vowel that is pronounced with its name. ⊶

cake	fact	game	life	tap	cup	test	home
these	left	bit	tune	spell	bag	drop	plane
mine	tube	soft	nose	kill	dust		

5   Repeat the words in the box in **4** and check your answers.

6   In the table on the next page, C stands for a consonant, V stands for a vowel and e is the letter 'e'. (C) stands for a *possible* consonant. So, for example, (C)CVCe can be CCVCe (as in the word 'drive') or CVCe (as in the word 'dive'); (C)CVC(C) can be CCVCC (as in the word 'clock') or CVCC (as in the word 'back'), and so on. ⊶

Using the examples in **4**, complete the table with example words, then complete the sentence to give you a rule about how to pronounce these vowel letters in most one-syllable words.

Pronunciation in words written

Vowel	(C)CVCe	(C)CVC(C)
a e i o u		

When a one-syllable word ends with ...., the vowel letter is pronounced with its name.

Unit 65 Pronouncing vowel pairs

In Unit 65 you will learn about the pronunciation of two vowel letters together (a vowel pair). Many vowel pairs can be pronounced in more than one way. For example:

'oa' is pronounced /əʊ/ in b<u>oa</u>t and /ɔ:/ in abr<u>oa</u>d;
'ei' is pronounced /eɪ/ in <u>ei</u>ght and /i:/ in rec<u>ei</u>ve.

1   Work in pairs. Complete the words below with one of these vowel pairs:

> 'ee'   'oo'   'ea'

1 thr......	5 betw.......n	9 eight......n	13 sch.......l
2 sp.......n	6 ch.......p	10 sl.......p	14 ......t
3 w.......l	7 aftern.......n	11 ......sy	15 alr.......dy
4 cl.......n	8 c......king	12 h.......vy	16 br.......k

2   Repeat the words and check your answers. ⊙─┓

3   Complete this table about the sixteen words in **1** to show how these vowel pairs are pronounced. Write in an *example* word for each pronunciation (e.g. spoon) and the *number of words* having that pronunciation (e.g. 3). Put a cross (✗) if the vowel pairs are not pronounced as shown at the top. ⊙─┓

	/i:/	/u:/	/e/	/ʊ/	/eɪ/
'ee'					
'oo'	✗	*spoon (3)*			
'ea'					

Pronouncing the vowel pair 'ou'

4 Listen to this conversation and write words from the box in the spaces. All the words contain the vowel pair 'ou'. 🔑

A: How was the holiday?

B: ....

A: Switzerland, wasn't it?

B: That's right. It's a beautiful ....

A: Did a .... of .... go?

B: No, just me and my ....

A: Where did you stay?

B: We rented a .... in Zurich.

A: How was the weather?

B: Well, a bit ....

A: Lots of shopping?

B: Oh, yes. Lots of .... And I .... this ....

A: Lovely. Did you go skiing, too?

B: Yes, we went .... to the ....

A: I've never been skiing. It .... too ....

B: Well, I had a few falls, but nothing too ....

A: And will you go back?

B: Probably. The only .... was, there were too many ....!
  But you've been on holiday, too, haven't you? How was ....?

A: Oh, we had a really good time …

trouble	yours	south
marvellous		blouse
cousin	serious	you
group	cloudy	sounds
mountains	dangerous	
country	souvenirs	
house	tourists	found

5 Repeat the words in the box in **4**. Then work in pairs and say the conversation together.

6 'ou' is pronounced in five different ways in these words. Group them and write them here. One word from each group is given. 🔑

1 marvellous ....

2 country ....

3 group ....

4 house ....

5 tourists ....

7   Work in pairs. Discuss what kind of holiday you prefer. Use some of these questions, but think of others if you can.

Do you prefer ...
1 to stay in your own country or go abroad?
2 to travel by boat or by coach?
3 to sleep a lot or to get up early and see lots of places?

Do you prefer staying in a place ...
4 near mountains or near the coast?
5 with dry but cool weather or wet but hot weather?
6 with a swimming pool or a beach?

Unit 66   Silent letters

1   Many words have letters that are not pronounced. Listen to these words and circle the letter in each word that is not pronounced. The first one is done for you. When you have finished, listen again and repeat the words. 🔑

> cupboard   climb   knee   island   half   autumn   know
> handkerchief   listen   knife   hour   two   Christmas
> answer   comb   honest   talk   handsome

2   In some other words letters are pronounced when the word is said slowly and carefully, but are not normally pronounced when the word is said in conversation.

Listen and repeat. These words are said twice: first, slowly and carefully, and then at normal speed. *Listen* to the words said slowly and *repeat* the words said at normal speed.

> interesting   police   chocolate   secretary   factory   several
> average   postman   different   family   government
> medicine   strawberries   aspirin   dustbin   favourite

3   Circle the letter in each word that is not pronounced at normal speed. 🔑

4 Repeat the sentences on the right. They all include a word from the box in **2**.

How often do you play football? •   • No, they're different.
Would you like some sweets? •   • I've already had some chocolate.
What's on the news? •   • Twice a week on average.
We've been robbed! •   • The government's resigned.
Who did you go on holiday with? •   • Strawberries and ice cream.
What shall we have for pudding? •   • Call the police.
What's in the bottle? •   • Several times.
What do you think of this cheese? •   • I went with my family.
Are these packets the same? •   • Some medicine for my cold.
Have you ever been to Paris? •   • It's my favourite.

5 Match the sentences on the left with the sentences on the right. Then work in pairs and say the conversations together. 🔑

6 Work in pairs to write similar conversations. Use the words given. One is done for you.

1 book   ... interesting
2 letters   ... postman
3 work   ... factory
4 headache ... aspirins
5 rubbish   ... dustbin
6 typed   ... secretary

*1 A: What's the book like?
    B: It's really interesting.*

Then say the conversations you have written to the rest of the class.

Key

This key consists of answers to the exercises and transcripts of the recordings where they do not appear in the unit.

Part 1 Vowels

Unit 2 The short vowels /æ/, /ɪ/ and /e/

3   A: Where were you st<u>a</u>nding?
B: Outside my fl<u>a</u>t.
A: Where was the m<u>a</u>n?
B: He r<u>a</u>n out of the b<u>a</u>nk.
A: Was he c<u>a</u>rrying anything?
B: A bl<u>a</u>ck b<u>a</u>g.
A: Th<u>a</u>nk you, m<u>a</u>dam.

5a   A: Th<u>i</u>s one?
B: A b<u>i</u>t b<u>i</u>g.
A: Let's g<u>i</u>ve her th<u>i</u>s one, then.
B: St<u>i</u>ll too b<u>i</u>g.
A: W<u>i</u>ll th<u>i</u>s f<u>i</u>t?

B: Yes, I th<u>i</u>nk so. Sh<u>e</u>'s quite th<u>i</u>n.

b   A: And can you g<u>e</u>t some <u>e</u>ggs?
B: How m<u>a</u>ny?
A: T<u>e</u>n, please.
B: <u>A</u>nything <u>e</u>lse?
A: Some br<u>ea</u>d. Do you need <u>a</u>ny money?
B: No, I'll pay by ch<u>e</u>que.

Unit 3 The short vowels /ɒ/, /ʊ/ and /ʌ/

2   watch/stopped   just/lunch   blood/cut
looks/good   got/cough   not/long
shut/stuck   pull/push   cook/book

4   1   A: What time is it?
B: Sorry, my <u>watch</u> has <u>stopped</u>.
2   A: Aren't you well?
B: No, I've <u>got</u> a <u>cough</u>.
3   A: What time's the bus?
B: <u>Not long</u> now.
4   A: Do you like it?
B: Yes, it <u>looks good</u>.
5   A: Can't you <u>shut</u> the door?
B: No, it's <u>stuck</u>.
6   A: Is that <u>blood</u>?
B: Yes, I <u>cut</u> my finger.
7   A: Is Tom here?
B: No, he's <u>just</u> gone for <u>lunch</u>.
8   A: What are you reading?
B: It's a <u>cook book</u>.
9   A: I can't open the door.
B: <u>Pull/Push</u> it, don't <u>push/pull</u> it!

6 Possible answers:
2 a good book, holiday, film
3 a comfortable bed, seat;
  comfortable shoes
4 a horrible dream,
  journey, picture
5 a funny TV programme,
  joke, story

Unit 4 /ɪ/ & /e/ and /æ/ & /ʌ/

3 1 Go to the <u>lift</u>, and then go up to the sixth floor. (A)
2 They <u>fell</u> in a hole in the road. (B)
3 You'll be late as <u>well</u>, Tom. (B)
4 You don't <u>spell</u> 'orange juice' like that. (B)
5 Wait <u>till</u> I come home. (A)
6 Can you <u>let</u> me have a cigarette? (B)
7 It was too expensive to buy <u>ten</u>. (B)
8 Can I have the <u>bill</u>, please? (A)

5

/æ/ + /ʌ/	/ʌ/ + /æ/	/ʌ/ + /ʌ/	/æ/ + /æ/
Stand up! A jazz club.	A hungry cat. A company manager. A gun factory.	Somewhere sunny. Hurry up! A lucky number. Nothing much.	A black jacket. A traffic jam. A plastic bag.

6 Most likely answers:
1 What did you do at the weekend?   Nothing much.
2 What's her job?   A company manager.
3 What was he wearing?   A black jacket.
4 Where did you go last night?   A jazz club.
5 Where do you work?   A gun factory.
6 Hurry up!   I'm coming as fast as I can!
7 What made you late?   A traffic jam.

Unit 5 The long vowels /iː/, /ɜː/, /ɑː/, /ɔː/ and /uː/

2 1 clean /iː/ visa, piece, me, free
2 bird   /ɜː/ prefer, early, Thursday, word
3 car   /ɑː/ heart, laugh, banana, half
4 four   /ɔː/ law, water, abroad, bought
5 food   /uː/ improve, fruit, June, blue

4 1 A: Have you <u>seen</u> my niece?
        B: Is she the girl in the <u>skirt</u>?
     2 A: Do you like my <u>blue</u> boots?
        B: I prefer the <u>purple</u> ones.
     3 A: When did you lose your <u>suitcase</u>?
        B: Last <u>March</u>.
     4 A: What did he do when he saw the <u>report</u>?
        B: He started to <u>laugh</u>.
     5 A: It's his birthday on the <u>third</u>, isn't it?
        B: Yes. I've bought him a <u>portable</u> TV.
     6 A: Where did your <u>father</u> leave the car?
        B: It's parked in the <u>car park</u>.

Unit 6 /æ/ & /ɑː/ and /ɪ/ & /iː/

1 | | | |
|---|---|---|
| 1 b<u>a</u>throom /æ/ | (B) | 7 p<u>a</u>ssport /ɑː/ (A) |
| 2 gl<u>a</u>sses /æ/ | (B) | 8 f<u>a</u>st /æ/ (B) |
| 3 d<u>a</u>nce /ɑː/ | (A) | 9 <u>a</u>fter /æ/ (B) |
| 4 <u>a</u>sk /ɑː/ | (A) | 10 p<u>a</u>st /æ/ (B) |
| 5 l<u>a</u>st /æ/ | (B) | 11 p<u>a</u>th /ɑː/ (A) |
| 6 <u>a</u>nswer /ɑː/ | (A) | 12 <u>a</u>fternoon /ɑː/ (A) |

3 Possible answers:

1	Things to eat	sweets and chicken
2	Numbers	fourteen and a million
3	Things containing water	river and stream
4	Jobs	builder and teacher
5	Parts of the body	knee and finger
6	Places where people live	street and city
7	Holiday times	Christmas and Easter
8	Countries	India and Egypt
9	Nationalities	Swedish and British
10	Things to drink	milk and tea

Unit 7 /ʌ/, /ʊ/ & /uː/ and /ɒ/ & /ɔː/

2

/ʌ/ e.g. sun	/ʊ/ e.g. would	/uː/ e.g. two
customer	full	include
gun	pull	supermarket
Sunday	put	June
number	push	flu

4 a) 6 & 2   b) 1 & 7   c) 8 & 3   d) 9 & 4   e) 10 & 5

5

       /ʊ/   /ʌ/
1 Where shall I p<u>u</u>t your l<u>u</u>ggage?

       /uː//uː/   /uː/
2 But I bought a n<u>ew</u> t<u>u</u>be on T<u>ue</u>sday.

   /uː/   /ʌ/   /ʌ/
3 It's t<u>oo</u> hot. It's a l<u>o</u>vely s<u>u</u>nny day.

    /ʌ/   /ʊ/   /uː/   /uː/   /uː/ /uː/
4 My <u>u</u>ncle. W<u>ou</u>ld y<u>ou</u> like me t<u>o</u> introd<u>u</u>ce y<u>ou</u>?

          /ʊ/ /ʊ/   /ʊ/
5 It's from a really g<u>oo</u>d c<u>oo</u>k b<u>oo</u>k.

       /ʌ/ /uː/
6 There isn't m<u>u</u>ch t<u>oo</u>thpaste left.

     /uː/   /ʌ/ /uː/
7 In the b<u>oo</u>t. There's j<u>u</u>st a s<u>ui</u>tcase.

     /ʊ/   /ʊ/   /ʌ/
8 I think I'll p<u>u</u>t on my w<u>oo</u>llen j<u>u</u>mper.

  /uː/   /uː//uː/
9 Wh<u>o</u>'s that in the bl<u>ue</u> s<u>ui</u>t?

    /ʌ/   /uː/   /ʌ/
10 That <u>o</u>nion s<u>ou</u>p was w<u>o</u>nderful.

Unit 8 The long vowels /eɪ/, /aɪ/, /əʊ/ and /aʊ/

2

	/eɪ/	/aɪ/	/əʊ/	/aʊ/
1	1	0	3	1
2	4	1	0	0
3	1	0	1	3
4	0	4	0	1
5	2	0	2	1
6	0	3	1	1

3   Text with correct version in brackets:
One morning last April (July), Joan was lying in bed when the doorbell (phone) rang. It was her friend, Dave, who invited her out for a picnic at the seaside. Later that day Jean (Joan) left her flat (house) and drove (rode) her car (bike) to the bus (railway) station to catch the bus (train). She was wearing a T-shirt and skirt (coat and trousers) as it was quite hot (cold). As she sat on the bus (train) she looked out of the door (window). The sun was shining (It was cloudy). She saw a plane going over a forest (mountain) and some horses (cows) in the fields. Before long she arrived at the river (seaside) and met Steve (Dave). They went down to the beach and had their picnic next to a rock (boat). They had sandwiches and crisps (cake and ice cream), and Steve (Dave) painted a picture (took some photos). They had a lovely day.

Unit 9 /eɪ/ & /e/ and /əʊ/ & /ɔː/

2 potato   dentist   Belgium   November   seven   eight   sailor
radio   train   Asia   May   sweater   Spain   yellow   table
grey   head   helicopter   South America   bed   embassy
bread   television   dress   brain   station

3 Possible answers:
potato + bread (things to eat)
dentist + sailor (jobs)
Belgium + Spain (countries)
November + May (months)
seven + eight (numbers)
radio + television (media/use electricity)
train + helicopter (means of transport)
Asia + South America (continents)
sweater + dress (items of clothing)
yellow + grey (colours)
table + bed (items of furniture)
head + brain (parts of the body)
embassy + station (buildings)

7 Words including /əʊ/ or /ɔː/ that could be used to describe the pictures:

Picture 1
A wardrobe in the corner with an open door; clothes inside the wardrobe; a coat on the back of the wardrobe door; man walking through bedroom door; girl at table, drawing; table with a drawer; ball on floor; window; snow through window.

Picture 2
Crossroads; men digging hole in road; coach; motorbike; post office, hotel, shop with 'Closed' sign; phone box; chimney with smoke coming out; it's autumn; it's a quarter past four; old man walking along – bald, wrapped up warmly against the cold.

Part 2 Consonants

Unit 10 /p/, /b/, /t/, /d/, /k/ and /g/

2 a) /k/ and /g/   b) /t/ and /d/   c) /p/ and /b/

3 Tom wants: some trousers, a tennis racket, a trumpet, a typewriter, a tent
Deborah wants: a dictionary, a desk, a dress, a dog
Kathy wants: a cat, a cake, a calendar, a clock, a camera
Gary wants: some gloves, a golf club
Pam wants: some perfume, a painting (or picture), a pen, a purse
Barbara wants: a blouse, a bracelet, a bookcase, a bicycle

Who wants most presents? *Tom*
Who wants fewest presents? *Gary*

Unit 11 /t/ & /d/ and /p/ & /b/

1 The words on the recording are:

1 president   2 pedestrian   3 midnight   4 introduce
5 industry   6 immediately   7 advertise   8 accident
9 granddaughter   10 stupid

Answers
1 b   2 b   3 b   4 a   5 b
6 b   7 b   8 b   9 b   10 a

3 a) 1 & 9   b) 7 & 2   c) 5 & 3   d) 4 & 6   e) 10 & 8

5 The most likely answers are:
a piece of pie; a bottle of perfume; a pair of pyjamas; a book of stamps; a box of pencils; a portion of chips; a bag of shopping; a basket of pears; a plate of pasta; a packet of biscuits; a bunch of grapes; a pile of bricks; a bar of soap.

Unit 12 /s/, /z/, /f/, /v/, /θ/ and /ð/

2 a) /f/ and /v/   b) /s/ and /z/   c) /θ/ and /ð/

4 1 b   2 b   3 a   4 b   5 a   6 a   7 a   8 b   9 b   10 a
11 a   12 b   13 a   14 b   15 b

Unit 13 /θ/ & /ð/ and /v/, /f/ & /b/

2 Most likely answers:

1 A: Where's the toilet?
  B: The bathroom's through there.
  A: Thanks.
  B: That's OK.

2 A: What time's the train to Doncaster?
  B: Three thirty.
  A: When does it get there?
  B: Ten twenty-three.

3 A: Is that Tom and David?
  B: Yes, they're always together.
  A: They're brothers, aren't they?
  B: That's right.

3 1 a   2 a   3 b   4 b   5 b   6 a   7 a   8 b   9 a   10 a

5 Most likely question and answer pairs are:

Where did Beverly …
watch television?	In the living room.
buy some traveller's cheques?	In the bank (*or* At a travel agent's).
book a holiday?	At a travel agent's.
buy a novel?	From a bookshop.
deliver a birthday card?	To her neighbour.
have a very long bath?	In the bathroom.
borrow some books?	From the library.
have a conversation with a bus driver?	On a bus.
buy some bananas?	At a fruit and vegetable shop.

Unit 14 /ʃ/, /tʃ/, /ʒ/ and /dʒ/

2 Most likely answers:
a) watch television?	In the lounge.
b) arrange a holiday?	At a travel agent's.
c) buy shoes?	At a shoe shop.
d) wash up?	In the kitchen.
e) keep cheese?	In the fridge.
f) learn a foreign language?	At college.
g) catch a coach?	At a coach station.
h) cash a cheque?	At a bank.
i) buy matches?	At a newsagent's.
j) keep a car?	In the garage.

5 The food and drink from the box in **3** that appear in the conversation are:

sugar   chips   chocolate   fish   fresh vegetables   porridge

Conversation on the recording:

P(atient): So how much do I have to lose, then?

D(octor): Well, Mr Taylor, I would suggest at least two stone.

P: Oh dear. How could I do that?

D: Well, let's look at what you're eating at the moment, shall we? Give me an idea of what sorts of things you eat during the day.

P: Well, I've got a very sweet tooth, I'm afraid. I eat a lot of sugar. I like chips a lot and I'm addicted to chocolate. I have to have a lot of chocolate.

D: I see.

P: Is that wrong?

D: Well, yes it is. I'm going to give you a diet sheet, and I recommend that you follow it. The most important things to put into your diet are fish, fresh vegetables and something like porridge for breakfast.

P: Oh, porridge. I like porridge.

D: Good.

P: Can I make it with milk …?

Unit 15 /ʃ/ & /tʃ/ and /dr/ & /tr/

2

	/ʃ/	/tʃ/		/ʃ/	/tʃ/
information	☑	☐	special	☑	☐
furniture	☐	☑	commercial	☑	☐
education	☑	☐	temperature	☐	☑
insurance	☑	☐	examination	☑	☐
suggestion	☐	☑	picture	☐	☑
profession	☑	☐	delicious	☑	☐
question	☐	☑	station	☑	☐

4 1 A: It's a really busy *street*.
B: Yes, there's always a lot of *traffic* and *pedestrians*.
2 A: Which *instruments* do you play?
B: The *trumpet* and the *drums*.
3 A: What *countries* would you most like to visit?
B: *Australia* and *Austria*.
4 A: Are you going to *drive*?
B: No, I'll *travel* by *train*.
5 A: Is her *dress dry* yet?
B: Yes, it's in the *wardrobe*.

Unit 16 /w/, /r/, /j/ and /l/

2 /w/ sounds are underlined. The 'w' letter that is not pronounced /w/ is circled.

A: What's the weather like?
B: Awful. It's wet and windy.
A: Shall we have a walk anyway?
B: Let's wait twenty minutes.

3 /j/ sounds are underlined. The 'y' letters that are not pronounced /j/ are circled.
The /j/ sounds not written with the letter 'y' are marked.

/j/
A: I had an interview yesterday.
B: Where?
/j/
A: At the Daily News.
B: Did you get the job?
A: I don't know yet.

4 /r/ sounds are underlined. The 'r' letters that are not pronounced /r/ are circled.

A: Did you remember to ring Ray?
B: I tried three times on Friday.
A: He was probably at work.
B: You're probably right. I'll try again tomorrow.

5 Conversation on the recording:

B(ob): Hello, Sarah.

S(arah): Hi, Bob.

B: You've been away, haven't you?

S: Yeah, I've had a lovely holiday. I went to Sweden.

B: Oh, great. Did you go on your own or …

S: No, I went with somebody I work with, a friend, yeah.

B: Fantastic. Where did you stay?

S: Well, it was in a very small place. I stayed in a small hotel. It was, you know, nothing luxurious, but it was clean and it was quiet.

B: Sounds great.

S: Yeah, it was lovely.

B: What did you get up to? Was there much to do out there?

S: Well, it's very sporty. We did a lot of swimming, and I tried windsurfing.

B: Oh, I've always wanted to do that.

S: Yeah, it's good.

B: Must have been good weather then?

S: Well, it wasn't very warm, but no, it was quite cool, but we were lucky it didn't rain. No, it was dry all the time.

B: Oh, great, you're looking fantastic.

Spaces in column A to be completed as follows:

Where?	Sweden
Who with?	with a friend
Hotel?	clean, quiet
Things to do?	windsurfing, swimming
Weather?	cool, dry

Unit 17 /w/ & /v/ and /r/ & /l/

2 1 2 I've only got twel<u>v</u>e.

2 1 She works hard e<u>v</u>ery day.

3 3 We had to dri<u>v</u>e up the pa<u>v</u>ement to a<u>v</u>oid him.

4 3 I've lost my wallet, tra<u>v</u>eller's cheques and <u>v</u>isa.

5 3 We're ha<u>v</u>ing <u>v</u>isitors o<u>v</u>er the weekend.

4 1 2 <u>W</u>hat's this <u>o</u>ne over here?

2 2 <u>W</u>as every piece of furniture made of <u>w</u>ood?

3 2 It's q<u>u</u>ite <u>w</u>arm for November.

4 3 They're having just a q<u>u</u>iet <u>w</u>edding next <u>W</u>ednesday.

5 4 It <u>w</u>as very <u>w</u>et last <u>w</u>eek, <u>w</u>asn't it?

5 Possible answers:

You might say …	but probably not …
a rich uncle	a rich letter
a slippery road	a slippery river
a musical instrument	a musical football
an electronic calculator	an electronic letter
a horrible brother	a horrible river
a dangerous road	a dangerous calculator
a difficult problem	a difficult bathroom
Australian football	an Australian bathroom
a clean bathroom	a clean uncle
a private road	a private flower
a lovely flower	a lovely problem
a favourite building	a favourite calculator

Unit 18 /m/, /n/ and /ŋ/

2
1 He's ironing.
2 He's listening to music.
3 He's painting.
4 He's studying English grammar.
5 He's shopping.
6 He's singing.
7 He's washing up.
8 He's cooking.
9 He's gardening.
10 He's playing tennis.

3
1 He likes ironing.
2 He doesn't like listening to music.
3 He likes painting.
4 He likes studying English grammar.
5 He doesn't like shopping.
6 He likes singing.
7 He doesn't like washing up.
8 He likes cooking.
9 He likes gardening.
10 He doesn't like playing tennis.

Part 3 Consonant clusters

Unit 19 Consonant letters and consonant sounds

2

	Number of consonant letters	Number of consonant sounds		Number of consonant letters	Number of consonant sounds
1 blood	2	2 (/bl/)	7 light	3	1 (/t/)
2 jump	2	2 (/mp/)	8 next	2	3 (/kst/)
3 ticket	2	1 (/k/)	9 there	2	1 (/ð/)
4 tablet	2	2 (/bl/)	10 report	2	1 (/t/)
5 dollar	2	1 (/l/)	11 film	2	2 (/lm/)
6 chair	2	1 (/tʃ/)	12 street	3	3 (/str/)

3 Possible answers:

	/l/	/m/	/r/
/k/	clock	✘	cross
/d/	✘	✘	dress
/g/	glass	✘	grapes
/p/	plug	✘	prize
/s/	slow	small	✘
/t/	✘	✘	triangle

Unit 20 Consonant clusters at the beginning of words

3
What did Sue have for Christmas?	A <u>bl</u>ue <u>bl</u>ouse.
How can I speak English better?	<u>Pr</u>actise your <u>pr</u>onunciation.
What do we need from the supermarket?	Just <u>br</u>ead and <u>cr</u>isps.
What should I take on my holiday to Iceland?	<u>Pl</u>enty of warm <u>cl</u>othes.
What's the weather like?	Quite <u>cl</u>oudy.

5
How many tickets do you want?	<u>Thr</u>ee, <u>pl</u>ease.
Where shall we meet?	At the <u>br</u>idge by the <u>st</u>ation.
What do you like best on TV?	<u>Thr</u>illers and <u>sp</u>orts <u>pr</u>ogrammes.
What did you buy in town?	A <u>cl</u>ock and some new <u>tr</u>ousers.
Oh no, I've missed it.	It's OK. There are <u>pl</u>enty more <u>tr</u>ains this evening.
He can't understand my English.	<u>Tr</u>y <u>sp</u>eaking more <u>sl</u>owly.

Unit 21 More on consonant clusters at the beginning of words

1
1. Is the <u>cl</u>ock broken?
2. They'll <u>gr</u>ow much higher than that.
3. He used to be a postman, but now he's a <u>dr</u>iver.
4. Shall we <u>p</u>ay now or later?
5. How much money did she <u>sp</u>end?
6. How many have you <u>b</u>ought?
7. The <u>pl</u>ane was terrible.
8. Are you sure it's <u>tr</u>ue?
9. Did you <u>s</u>ay two weeks or three?
10. What <u>sp</u>ort do you like best?

3
1 a dress   2 a frying pan   3 flippers   4 a swimming costume
5 gloves   6 a clock   7 a sweater   8 a sleeping bag   9 a scarf
10 a ski suit   11 swimming trunks   12 skis   13 a plate   14 a spade
15 slippers

4 Conversation on the recording:

A: Oh, Andrew.

B: Hello.

A: I wanted to ask you a couple of questions. I'm going on holiday skiing soon and I wanted to ask you what you think I should take. Obviously, I've got to take a ski suit and gloves.

B: Yes, you'll need gloves. You'll definitely need those. If you've got your own skis, too, that could save you a lot of money because otherwise you have to hire them and it's quite expensive. Where are you going to stay?

A: Oh, I'm staying in a hotel. Quite a big one, I think.

B: Well, in that case I should take your swimming costume because most of these big hotels they have indoor pools nowadays …

A: That's a good idea.

B: … it's really relaxing, you know, having a swim after skiing all day.

A: Andrew, do you think I'll be warm enough in a ski suit? I mean, without a jacket on top?

B: I should think so, yes. I mean, if you've got your ski suit and a couple of warm sweaters, and a scarf perhaps. Yeah, you should be OK with that.

A: So no jacket …

Unit 22 Consonant clusters at the end of words

1 On recording:
since, want, garden, friend, happen, silence, haven't, understand, pronounce, listen, thousand, once, important, conversation, orange, find, direction, different, eleven

2

/n/ + /s/	/n/ + /t/	/n/ + /d/
since	want	friend
silence	haven't	understand
pronounce	important	thousand
once	different	find

3

How long have you been here?	<u>Since</u> Wednesday.
Do you <u>want</u> one?	No, thanks.
Aren't they the same?	No, they're <u>different</u>.
How often do you come?	<u>Once</u> a week.
Is this your sister?	No, my <u>friend</u>.
You've taken my coat!	No, I <u>haven't</u>.

5 Likely answers:

Things you can eat or drink: toast, beans, orange, milk, chips

Animals: elephant, beetle, wasp, fox, ant

Parts of the body: waist, ankle, wrist, tongue, chest

People: adult, child, yourself, parents, boyfriend

Ways people feel: pleased, terrible, amused, depressed

Unit 23 More on consonant clusters at the end of words

3 1 A: Where's your <u>cousin</u>?
       B: She's in <u>hospital</u>.
       A: What's the <u>trouble</u>?
       B: She fell off her <u>bicycle</u>.

    2 A: When's the <u>examination</u>?
       B: At <u>eleven</u>.
       A: How do you feel?
       B: <u>Terrible</u>.

    3 A: What's in this <u>bottle</u>?
       B: A <u>chemical</u>.
       A: What's it for?
       B: Something <u>special</u>!

    4 A: Press that <u>button</u>.
       B: This one in the <u>middle</u>?
       A: Yes.
       B: What'll <u>happen</u>?
       A: Just <u>listen</u>.

Unit 24 Consonant clusters in the middle of words

1 The words given are suggestions (for English only):

Beginning	Middle	End
✓ stop	cus<u>t</u>omer	✓ last
✗	seve<u>n</u>teen	✓ went
✗	Dece<u>m</u>ber	✗
✗	shoul<u>d</u>er	✓ old
✓ <u>p</u>rize	A<u>p</u>ril	✗
✗	com<u>p</u>any	✓ lump
✗	bla<u>n</u>ket	✓ bank
✗	en<u>v</u>elope	✗

3 1 passport   2 loudly   3 taxi   4 quietly   5 husband   6 painting
    7 businessman   8 doctor   9 aeroplane   10 boyfriend

5 1 Cities: Oslo, Bombay, London
    2 Months: April, December, October
    3 Pieces of furniture: wardrobe, armchair, bookshelf
    4 Things to eat: apple pie, chocolates, biscuits, cornflakes
    5 Things that use electricity: toaster, tape recorder, computer
    6 Buildings: library, hospital, post office, bookshop

Unit 25 Consonant clusters across words

2 orange juice, arrival time, capital city, classical music, film star, girlfriend, left-handed, portable television

4 1 (b) (People talking about some photographs one of them has taken)
    2 (d) (Students talking about their homework)
    3 (a) (People talking about a pop concert)
    4 (c) (People talking about a missing car)

Unit 26 More on consonant clusters across words

2 She was wearing her red dress at the party.
We lost the match one nil.
Five visitors came to see us yesterday.
They had a team meeting after the game.
Is there enough food for the party?
A bad dream woke me up.
There's some money in my purse.
It takes five minutes.

4 1 cold   2 pleased   3 that   4 contact   5 fact   6 visit   7 friend
8 can't

6 1 That's true.
2 I don't know yet.
3 Help yourself.
4 It's very pretty.
5 Please try.

6 Can you come tomorrow?
7 Can I have some more?
8 Thanks very much.
9 But it's so expensive.

7 Most likely answers:

a) 4, 9, 1
b) 6, 2, 5
c) 7, 3, 8

Part 4 Stress and rhythm

Unit 27 Syllables and stress

2 furniture 3   bought 1   blackboard 2   examination 5   remember 3
collect 2   anybody 4   please 1   grandmother 3   impossible 4
electricity 5   rabbit 2   directions 3   goodbye 2

4

furniture   bought   blackboard   examination   remember   collect

anybody   please   grandmother   impossible   electricity   rabbit

directions   goodbye

5

Budapest   Bangkok   Madrid   Moscow   Jakarta   Lima

Unit 28 Patterns of stress in words

2 The odd one out in each list is:

1 chicken   2 Japan   3 telephone   4 policeman   5 supermarket

3

A single or return?   I was hoping to invite you.

I'm a stranger here myself.   I'll be busy, I'm afraid.

Have you ever been abroad?   I'd like a ticket to Madrid.

Is the station far away?   I went to Brazil in April.

4 Best answers:

I'd like a ticket to Madrid.	A single or return?
Is the station far away?	I'm a stranger here myself.
I was hoping to invite you.	I'll be busy, I'm afraid.
Have you ever been abroad?	I went to Brazil in April.

Unit 29 More practice; stress patterns in numbers

1 economics 4   Zimbabwe 3   diplomat 3   July 2   Chinese 2
biology 4   Arabic 3   Peru 2   August 2   photographer 4
Norwegian 3   Germany 3   accountant 3   chemistry 3   September 3

2 1 accountant   2 August   3 biology   4 Norwegian   5 Zimbabwe

3 1 11.14   2 50   3 16   4 17   5 £2.80   6 £90

The sentences on the recording are:
1 The next train to arrive at this platform is the 11.14 to Birmingham.
2 I've got a very old car. It can only go at 50 kilometres per hour.
3 We could meet in my office. It's number 16.
4 My brother is 35, but his wife is 17!
5 It's very good, and it only cost £2.80.
6 I once stayed in a hotel in London which cost £90 a night.

Unit 30 Finding out about stress patterns

1 carry (V)   famous (A)   daughter (N)   husband (N)   forget (V)
lovely (A)   yellow (A)   prefer (V)   frighten (V)   kitchen (N)
ugly (A)   mountain (N)

2

| ○ ∘ | ○ ∘ | ○ ∘ | ○ ∘ | ∘ ○ | ○ ∘ | ○ ∘ |
| carry | famous | daughter | husband | forget | lovely | yellow |

| ∘ ○ | ○ ∘ | ○ ∘ | ○ ∘ | ○ ∘ |
| prefer | frighten | kitchen | ugly | mountain |

3 Most <u>nouns</u> and <u>adjectives</u> are stressed on the first syllable. Some <u>verbs</u> are stressed on the first syllable and others on the second.

5

○ ∘	∘ ○	○ ∘ ∘	∘ ○ ∘
garden	machine	motorbike	museum
also	July	photograph	suggestion
	across	ambulance	professor
	perhaps		

Unit 31 Pronouncing unstressed syllables

3

○ ∘	∘ ○ ∘∘	∘ ○ ∘	○ ∘
1 answ<u>er</u>	5 Austr<u>a</u>lian (or Australi<u>a</u>n)		9 wom<u>a</u>n

| ∘ ○ ∘ | ○ ∘ | | ∘ ○ ∘ |
| 2 import<u>a</u>nt | 6 dist<u>a</u>nt | | 10 comput<u>er</u> |

| ○ ∘ ∘ ∘ | ○ ∘ | | ∘ ○ ∘∘ |
| 3 calc<u>u</u>lat<u>or</u> | 7 weath<u>er</u> | | 11 <u>A</u>meric<u>a</u>n |

| ○ ∘∘ | ○ ∘ | | ○ ∘ |
| 4 visit<u>or</u> | 8 mirr<u>or</u> | | 12 pregn<u>a</u>nt |

Unit 32 Rhythm

3
1 A bottle <u>of</u> milk.
2 I'll go <u>and</u> see.
3 I've nothing <u>to</u> say.
4 A hundred <u>and</u> forty.
5 I'm going <u>to</u> London.
6 I have <u>to</u> go.

7 A piece <u>of</u> cake.
8 The first <u>of</u> October
9 My mother <u>and</u> father.
10 I've lots <u>to</u> do.
11 A type <u>of</u> bread.
12 What's six <u>and</u> eight?

5 fish and chips   bread and butter   cheese and biscuits   coffee and cake
apple pie and cream

Unit 33 More on rhythm

2
2...	What did he say?	Five pounds an hour.	2...
1...	Shall we dance?	I'll call the police.	3...
2...	What do you earn?	He told me to rest.	3...
2...	Here is your change.	Thanks very much.	2...
1...	Where's it gone?	On the roof.	1...
2...	Give me your purse.	Yes, of course.	1...

3

What did he say?	He told me to rest.
Shall we dance?	Yes, of course.
What do you earn?	Five pounds an hour.
Here is your change.	Thanks very much.
Where's it gone?	On the roof.
Give me your purse.	I'll call the police.

Unit 34 Rhythm and moving stress

1 Conversation on the recording:

A: Do you want to see a photo of the English class I've been teaching?

B: Mmm. That's a good photo, isn't it? They look a very mixed group of students.

A: Yes, they are. They're all from different countries – all European and Asian, though.

B: So where are they all from?

A: Well, you've met Tomo, haven't you?

B: Yes, he was at the party, wasn't he?

A: Yes, that's right. He's a doctor. He's Japanese. Well, you can see him at the back on the right.

B: Yes, I recognise him.

A: And the other three students along the back are a journalist – she's Swedish. That's the one next to Tomo.

B: I see.

A: And then next to her is a dentist. She's Chinese.

B: They've got lots of different jobs, haven't they?

A: Amazing variety. At the back on the left is a diplomat. She's Spanish. Very important, too, I think.

B: Really?

A: Then next to her is a businessman. He's Taiwanese. Then at the front on the left is a teacher. He's Norwegian.

B: And then who are the two on the other side of Tomo?

A: Well, the woman next to Tomo is an actress. She's Italian. And then at the front next to her is a farmer. He's Portuguese.

Japanese – doctor	Taiwanese – businessman
Swedish – journalist	Norwegian – teacher
Chinese – dentist	Italian – actress
Spanish – diplomat	Portuguese – farmer

2 Japanese   Swedish   Chinese   Spanish   Taiwanese

Norwegian   Italian   Portuguese

4
1 Japanese ✓
2 Swedish ✗
3 Chinese ✓
4 Spanish ✗
5 Taiwanese ✓
6 Norwegian ✗
7 Italian ✗
8 Portuguese ✓

Part 5 Sounds in connected speech

Unit 35 Slow speech and connected speech

1 & 2 On the recording (answers to **1** in bold):
   1 A: Can you see my briefcase?   B: **It's over there.**
   2 A: How many men were in the car?   B: **There were five of them.**
   3 A: What time is it?   B: **Ten past seven.**
   4 A: Can you help me open this bottle, please?   B: **Can't you do it?**
   5 A: When will you arrive?   B: **As soon as I can.**
   6 A: Excuse me, have you taken my coat by mistake?   B: **I don't think so.**
   7 A: Have you seen the film?   B: **Yeah, it's quite good.**
   8 A: You don't look very well.   B: **I've got a cold.**
   9 A: Well, are we going to the theatre?   B: **I thought you said 'no'.**
  10 A: When are you going to clean the car?   B: **Perhaps I could do it tomorrow.**

3 a) 8   b) 2   c) 4   d) 1   e) 5   f) 6   g) 3   h) 7

4
a) What do you do?
b) What have you got there?
c) Have you got a light?
d) Have you been here long?
e) Where are you going?
f) What's the matter?
g) Do you know him?
h) What time is it?

Unit 36 Common words and phrases in connected speech

1 1 or   2 an   3 and   4 or   5 are   6 of   7 Are   8 of
   9 a   10 have

3 Before a word that begins with a consonant sound 'are', 'of' and 'or' are usually pronounced /ə/. Before a word that begins with a vowel sound, they are usually pronounced /ər /, /əv/ and /ər/.

4 1 A: **Excuse me.** B: Yes, what can I do for you?
2 A: What is it? B: **I don't know.**
3 A: What time is it? B: (It's) **About eight** (o'clock).
4 A: **Thank you.** B: **That's all right.**
5 A: **Are you going to go?** B: **Yes.**

5 1 ... want to ...
2 ... got to ...
3 Because ...
4 ... going to get you ... going to meet you ...
5 You've got to teach them about ...

Unit 37 Linking words together: Consonant + Vowel

4 Suggested answers:
1 a crowd of people   2 a map of the world   3 a box of matches
4 a bunch of flowers   5 a block of flats   6 a couple of hours
7 a piece of cake   8 a chest of drawers

5 Suggested answers:
1 You put up an umbrella.
2 You put out a light.
3 You put on your clothes.
4 You take off your clothes.
5 You take up golf (or any sport or hobby).
6 You turn off the radio; a light; the cooker.
7 You turn up the radio; the cooker.
8 You get on a bus.
9 You get in a car.
10 You keep off the grass.

Unit 38 Linking words together: Vowel + Consonant

3 Suggested answers:
post office, customs officer, headache, smoke alarm, travel agent, shop assistant, North Africa, musical instrument

4 Suggested answers:
sore throat, power station, Sahara Desert, flower shop, company director, computer keyboard, motorbike, letterbox

Unit 39 Linking words together: Consonant + Consonant

1 1 might   2 clean   3 felt   4 rained   5 want   6 need
7 thin   8 third   9 begin

Unit 40 Sounds that link words: /w/ and /j/ ('y')

1 Conversation on the recording:

Alan: Do you know it's Phil's birthday on Thursday?
Sue: I'd forgotten all about it.
Alan: I suppose we should buy him a present.
Sue: And we really ought to have a party for him.
Alan: Well, what can we get him?
Sue: It depends how much we want to pay.
Alan: If we pay about £10 we could get him something really nice.
Sue: What about a new umbrella. He's got that old blue one, but it's all broken. He should throw it away.
Alan: That's a great idea. And it won't be too expensive. And what about a party?
Sue: Well, we could invite a few friends around here. How about Thursday evening?
Alan: We could, but I know he's got an interview on Friday, and he might want to get ready for that.
Sue: Well, let's wait till the weekend. Anyway, more people will be free on Saturday.
Alan: OK. I'll buy the present, and you arrange the party.
Sue: Fine.

Answers:
1 On Thursday.   2 An umbrella.   3 On Saturday.

6 1 Who are you?
          w

   2 Germany imports gold.
              y

   3 Don't argue about it.
               w

   4 Coffee or tea?
            y

   5 I've been to Amsterdam.
               w

   6 Tomorrow afternoon.
              w

   7 Go away!
        w

   8 Hello, Ann!
          w

   9 Goodbye, Ann.
            y

   10 They weigh about five kilos.
                y

Unit 41 Sounds that link words: /r/

3 1 Is the **door** open?
   2 They've forgotten **their** air tickets.
   3 She's my **mother**-in-law.
   4 He started his new job a **year** ago.
   5 I've been waiting for an **hour** and a half.
   6 My **brother** is older than me.
   7 Do you live **far** away?
   8 **Neither** am I.

4 Suggested answers:

October/November   mother/father   under/over   summer/winter
before/after   near/far   brother/sister   here/there   sooner/later
car/helicopter   beer/water

Unit 42 Short sounds and sounds that are missed out

2   1 across   2 agree   3 arrive   4 awake   5 abroad   6 afraid
    7 alone   8 about   away

4   1   A: Is that ~~K~~im over there?
        B: <u>Who</u>?
        A: The man ~~who~~ took your <u>hand</u>bag?

    2   A: <u>He</u> wasn't at <u>home</u>.
        B: No, I think ~~h~~e's on <u>holiday</u>.

    3   A: <u>How</u>'s Tom these days?
        B: Didn't you <u>hear</u> about ~~h~~is <u>heart</u> attack?

    4   A: It says <u>here</u>, the Queen's coming.
        B: Where?
        A: <u>Here</u>.
        B: I do <u>hope</u> we'll be able to see ~~h~~er.

    5   A: What are you children fighting about?
        B: It's MY book.
        A: <u>HIS</u> book's over there.
        B: <u>HER</u> book's over there. This one's mine!

5   him, who, he('s), his, her
    'h' *is* pronounced when these words are at the start of a sentence.

Part 6 Intonation

Unit 43 Prominent words

1   1 (Thank) you.   6 It's a (lovely) place.
    2 I'm (tired.)   7 She's in the (sitting) room.
    3 (Chris) did.   8 It's (raining) again.
    4 It's getting (late.)   9 He's a (postman).
    5 I'm (sure) she will.   10 We had a (great) time.

3   a) 3   b) 1   c) 10   d) 8   e) 6   f) 9   g) 2   h) 4
    i) 7   j) 5

5   Suggested answers:
    chicken pie/salad/omelette/soup; tomato salad/omelette/soup; cheese
    salad/omelette; cherry pie; apple pie

8 Conversation on the recording:

Waitress: Are you ready to order now?
Customer: Yes, I think so.
Waitress: What will you have for a starter?
Customer: I think I'll have some soup. Tomato soup.
Waitress: Tomato soup. And what will you have for a main course?
Customer: I'd like a salad. Chicken salad.
Waitress: Chicken salad. OK. And what will you have for a dessert?
Customer: Mm. Let me see. I'll have some pie, please. Cherry pie.
Waitress: Cherry pie. OK. Thank you.

Unit 44 Repeated words and prominence

3 b

On the recording:
In the middle of the picture is a big circle, and just above it is a small circle. On the left of the big circle is a small triangle, and on the right is a big triangle.

4   In the middle   is a <u>big circle</u>.
       Above it   is a <u>small</u> circle.

       On the left of the big circle   is a <u>small triangle</u>.
       On the right   is a <u>big</u> triangle.

The repeated words are not made prominent.

Unit 45 More on prominent and non-prominent words

2   1 them   2 him   3 her   4 there   5 he   6 one   7 there
       8 us

4   Most likely answers:
       1 packet   2 bunch   3 jar   4 loaf   5 tin   6 bottle   7 jar
       8 packet/box   9 bunch   10 carton

Unit 46 Falling and rising tones

3   1 a) I went to London …   (↘)   (b) … on Saturday.   (↗)
       2 a) David …   (↗)   (b) … works in a bookshop. (↘)
       3 a) There's some cake … (↘)   (b) … in the kitchen.   (↗)
       4 a) In Hong Kong …   (↘)   (b) … last year.   (↘)
       5 a) I'm fairly sure …   (↗)   (b) … it's upstairs.   (↘)
       6 a) Yes, …   (↘)   (b) … of course.   (↘)
       7 a) Turn left here …   (↗)   (b) … then go straight on. (↘)
       8 a) Oh dear, …   (↘)   (b) … I *am* sorry.   (↘)
       9 a) I like it …   (↗)   (b) … very much.   (↘)
       10 a) I don't smoke …   (↘)   (b) … thank you.   (↘)

5 a) 2   b) 3   c) 1   d) 9   e) 5   f) 10   g) 7   h) 6
i) 4   j) 8

Unit 47 Reasons for falling and rising

2 3 I'm flying (↗) at ten o'clock (↘).
4 I've known him (↗) for years (↘).
5 I've been learning French (↗) for six years (↘).
6 Tuesday (↘) was the last time I saw him (↗).
7 Press the red one (↘), not the black one (↗).
8 Your papers (↗) are on the table (↘) in the kitchen (↘).

4 Falling tones are used in 'red' and 'blue' as they are information being given. A rising tone is used for 'my favourite' as the idea of favourites is already being talked about.

Unit 48 A second rising tone

1 1 b   2 a   3 c   4 a   5 b   6 b   7 a   8 b   9 c   10 a

2 1 S   2 D   3 D   4 D   5 D   6 S   7 S   8 D

3 1 B: YES ↘ – I'd LOVE to. ↘
2 B: NO ↘ – NOT YET. ↗
3 B: YES ↘ – I THINK so. ↗
4 B: NO ↘ – not REALLY. ↗
5 B: BYE ↗ – see you TOMORROW. ↗
6 B: PERHAPS ↗ – I don't KNOW yet. ↗
7 B: REALLY ↗ – I THOUGHT they would. ↗
8 B: on SUNDAY ↘ – IF the WEATHER'S good. ↗

Unit 49 Tonic words

3 a) It's on (top) of the bookcase.   d) At five (past) one.
b) With (milk), please.   e) It's on top of the (bookcase).
c) At (five) past one.   f) (With) milk, please.

5 1 f   2 c   3 e   4 b   5 a   6 d

7 1 A: Can I HELP you?
B: I'm looking for a DRESS.
A: They're on the SECOND floor.
B: THANK you.

2 A: What do you THINK?
B: I don't like the COLOUR.
A: I thought you LIKED red.
B: I prefer BLUE.

3 A: Shall we eat HERE?
  B: Let's sit over THERE.
  A: Under THAT tree?
  B: The OTHER one.

Unit 50 Predicting tones

2 1 A: Was it EXPENSIVE?

    B: QUITE expensive.

    A: How MUCH?

    B: A thousand POUNDS.

  2 A: Is it still RAINING?

    B: I THINK so.

    A: HEAVILY?

    B: Not VERY.

  3 A: What's on TV tonight?

    B: A HORROR film.

    A: Is it GOOD?

    B: I've HEARD it is.

Part 7 Sounds and grammar

Unit 51 Weak and strong forms; short and long forms

3 1 Do you like it?   Yes, very much.
    2 Can we go now?   A bit later.
    3 Does he live here?   No, next door.
    4 Can I take two?   Yes, of course.
    5 Does it hurt?   Not really.
    6 When do you go back?   Tomorrow.
    7 Why does she want to leave? She's tired.
    8 Where can we see one?   In a zoo.
    9 How do you feel now?   Much better.

Unit 52 Long and short forms of verbs

2 A: <u>I'd</u> like some of those apples, please. How much <u>are they</u>?
B: <u>They're</u> twelve pence each. How many <u>would you</u> like?
A: <u>I'll</u> have five, please.
B: There you are. <u>Shall I</u> put them in a bag for you?
A: Oh, <u>would you</u>? <u>That's</u> very kind of you.
B: Anything else?
A: No, <u>that's</u> all thanks. How much <u>is that</u>?
B: <u>That'll</u> be 60 pence, please.
A: <u>Here's</u> a £5 note.
B: <u>Have you</u> got anything smaller?
A: Er… oh, yes. <u>I've</u> got a pound coin.

4 The LONG form of these verbs is used in <u>questions</u>.

Unit 53 More on the long and short forms of verbs

1
How old are you?	I'm twenty-one.
Is she here?	No, she's in town.
When will you go?	I'll go tomorrow.
Shall we eat now?	I'd rather wait until later.
Have you been before?	Yes, I've been twice.

3
What's your name?	It's Rachel Jones.
When're they going?	They've got to be home by 11.
What's Jim got?	It's a present.
Where've you been?	I'm sorry. The train was late.
What're you doing?	I'm making dinner.

4 On the recording:

Mrs Jones: …They're called Tom and Paul. Tom's five and Paul's seven. Tom's wearing football shorts and Paul's got jeans on, I think. They're both wearing T-shirts, and I think Tom's got a jacket with him. Tom's got fair hair and Paul's got dark hair – oh, but he's probably wearing a hat. And they've got their dog with them. And … oh, thank goodness … they've just walked through the door…

Picture (b) is Tom and picture (d) is Paul.

Unit 54 Weak and strong forms of some conjunctions

2 1 a) Milk <u>but</u> no sugar.
   b) Milk <u>and</u> no sugar.
 2 a) Paul <u>and</u> Alison.
   b) Paul <u>or</u> Alison.
 3 a) It was small <u>but</u> very heavy.
   b) It was small <u>and</u> very heavy.
 4 a) Jean <u>and</u> her friend.
   b) Jean <u>or</u> her friend.
 5 a) <u>But</u> I want to go.
   b) <u>And</u> I want to go.
 6 a) Red <u>or</u> green.
   b) Red <u>and</u> green.

4 On recording and answers:
 1 In January, London is colder than Athens. (T)
 2 In July, Paris is about as wet as London. (T)
 3 In July, Stockholm is sunnier than Athens. (F)
 4 In January, Moscow is as sunny as Stockholm. (T)
 5 In July, Athens is hotter than Moscow. (T)
 6 In January, Paris is about the same temperature as Stockholm. (F)
 7 In January, Stockholm is colder than London. (T)
 8 In July, London is sunnier than Paris. (F)

Unit 55 Weak and strong forms of some prepositions

1 & 2 Answers to **2** underlined:
 1 He was looking .... the children in the park. [<u>for</u>/at]
 2 I was at home .... six o'clock. [<u>at</u>/from]
 3 They drove .... Glasgow last night. [<u>from</u>/to]
 4 He had a drawing .... Rome. [<u>of</u>/from]
 5 She picked up the ball and threw it .... her brother. [<u>at</u>/to]
 6 Do you like this picture? It's a present .... Sue. [<u>for</u>/from]
 7 The people .... France drink a lot of wine. [<u>of</u>/from]
 8 She pointed .... the ship. [<u>to</u>/at]

5 1 S   2 W   3 W   4 S   5 S   6 W   7 S   8 S   9 W
 10 S

6 Strong forms are used:
 a) when the prepositions end a sentence (examples 1, 4, 5, 8 and 10), and
 b) when they contrast with another preposition (example 7).

7 On recording:

From my home in Birmingham, first I'm going to the north of England. I'm going to stay in Durham at the Cumbria Hotel. I'm going to stay there for three days. Then I'm going to drive from Durham to Cambridge. I'm going to stay at the Monarch Hotel for two days. Then I'm going to drive to the west of England. I'm going to stay at the Clifton Guest House in Bristol for three days. From Bristol I'm going to drive to Brighton and stay at the Promenade Hotel for two days. After that I'm going to drive home again.

Unit 56 The pronunciation of '-ed' endings

1 On recording: (Jane Bradbury – JB; Friend – FR):

JB: I saw a terrible accident last week.

FR: Why, what <u>happened</u>?

JB: Well, I was working in my office. I <u>wanted</u> to see what the weather was like so I <u>walked</u> over to the window and I <u>looked</u> outside.

FR: And what did you see?

JB: Well, nothing at first. But then a car came along the road. It <u>stopped</u> at the crossing opposite my office. A man and a woman <u>started</u> to cross when another car drove straight over the crossing without even slowing down.

FR: Oh, no! Was anybody hurt?

JB: Well, the woman <u>jumped</u> out of the way and the car just <u>missed</u> her. But it <u>knocked</u> down the man.

FR: So what did you do?

JB: Well, after that I <u>phoned</u> for an ambulance and the police and then I went outside.

FR: Did it take long for them to come?

JB: No, they <u>arrived</u> in just two or three minutes. The ambulance men <u>helped</u> the woman to stand up. I think she was OK. But they <u>carried</u> the man into the ambulance on a stretcher. I <u>explained</u> what I'd seen to the police.

FR: And what about the driver?

JB: Well, apparently they <u>arrested</u> a man for dangerous driving.

The headline 'Man injured by car on crossing' best summarises what happened.

4

/t/	/d/	/ɪd/
walked	explained	wanted
knocked	phoned	arrested
jumped	arrived	started
looked		carried
stopped		
helped		
missed		

Unit 57 More on the pronunciation of '-ed' endings

1 1 rained 2 dropped 3 polluted 4 arrived / posted 5 finished
6 passed 7 laughed 8 mended 9 washed 10 walked

3 The additions to the table are indicated below:

/t/	/d/	/ɪd/
k p s gh (pronounced /f/) sh	n v	t d

4 Example story on recording:

One day Tom woke up and realised that he was late for work. He washed, shaved and brushed his teeth. He hurried downstairs and walked quickly to the bus stop. He waited for about five minutes before the bus arrived. But when he got to his office he discovered that it was closed. Tom had forgotten that it was Sunday!

Unit 58 The pronunciation of '-s' endings

2 Answers and pronunciation of endings:

		Odd one out	
1 looks, sleeps, cuts, hopes	(ending = /s/)	runs	(ending = /z/)
2 finishes, chooses, switches, washes	(/ɪz/)	includes	(/z/)
3 phones, gives, cleans, buys	(/z/)	teaches	(/ɪz/)
4 plays, stays, rains, happens	(/z/)	gets	(/s/)
5 forgets, sits, speaks, stops	(/s/)	touches	(/ɪz/)
6 begins, drives, seems, sells	(/z/)	promises	(/ɪz/)

3 The completed table should look like this:

/z/	/s/	/ɪz/
n d v y m ll	k p t	sh s, ch

5 Add 'g' under /z/ and 'dg' under /ɪz/.

6 Possible answers:
  Newsagent's – cigarettes, matches
  Shoe shop – shoes, slippers
  Clothes shop – jeans, socks, gloves
  Sweet shop – sweets
  Supermarket – biscuits, cornflakes
  Baker's – cakes
  Hardware shop – nails
  Greengrocer's – potatoes

Part 8 Pronouncing written words

Unit 59 Letters and sounds

2

	S	D		S	D		S	D
fog	☑	☐	winter	☐	☑	not	☑	☐
luck	☐	☑	shut	☐	☑	thin	☐	☑
cough	☐	☑	chess	☐	☑	other	☐	☑
cut	☑	☐	bill	☐	☑	touch	☐	☑
plan	☑	☐	dust	☑	☐			

3 b ☐1   f ☐1   k ☐1   n ☐1   s ☐2   w ☐1
   c ☐2   g ☐2   l ☐1   p ☐1   t ☐1
   d ☐1   h ☐1   m ☐1   r ☐1   v ☐1

Three letters are commonly pronounced in one of two ways:
'c' can be pronounced /k/ (cat) or /s/ (police)
'g' can be pronounced /g/ (gram) or /dʒ/ (age)
's' can be pronounced /s/ (spin) or /z/ (visa)

Unit 60 Pronouncing consonant letters 'c' and 'g'

3 a) The traffi©'s bad in the city centre.
   b) After the cinema, we went to a dis©o.
   c) I've been to Ameri©a twice.
   d) Only take this medicine in an emergency.
   e) I went a©ross the road to the post office.
   f) I had to ©olle©t a parcel.
   g) I haven't had a cigarette since December.
   h) ©all the police!

4 The letter 'c' is pronounced /s/ before the letters 'e', 'i' or 'y' in a word, and
   pronounced /k/ everywhere else.

5 The exceptions are:
   together, girl, begin, give, get

Unit 61 Pronouncing 'th'

3

How many are there?	A thousand.
What's the matter?	I'm thirsty.
Is this yours?	Yes, thank you.
What time's their train?	At three twenty-five.
Where are they?	Through here.
Is he fatter than me?	No, he's thinner.
What day are you going there?	On Thursday.

4 When 'th' is at the end of a word it is pronounced /θ/.

5 'th' is pronounced /ð/ in: father, other, weather, together, either, and rather.
'th' in the middle of a word is usually pronounced /ð/ if the word ends in 'er'.

7 Answers:
Josef Stalin died – 5th March 1953; State of Malaysia was created – 16th September 1963; Mrs Thatcher became Prime Minister – 3rd May 1979; John McEnroe won Wimbledon – 3rd July 1983; Pablo Picasso died – 8th April 1973; the first football World Cup began in Uruguay – 13th July 1930.

Unit 62 Pronouncing 'sh', 'ch' and 'gh'

2
1 one
2 machine
3 Possible answers: tough, rough, cough, laugh
4 Possible answers: night, high
5 ghost

3 Possible answers:
1 shampoo, toothbrush
2 cheese, fish
3 shoes, shirt
4 washing machine, dishwasher
5 shiver, cough
6 shop, church
7 ship, fish
8 tough, fresh
9 Chinese, British
10 rough, sharp

Unit 63 Pronunciation, spelling and word stress

3 daughter   camera   company   condition   petrol   neighbour
handsome   abroad   England   doctor   pronunciation

5 supper   suppose   commercial   common   collect   collar
concert   continue   person   percent

6 /ə/ is the common pronunciation of <u>unstressed</u> syllables. It is never the vowel sound in <u>stressed</u> syllables.

7 Answers (the /ə/ vowel in each word is underlined):
<u>a</u>dvertis<u>e</u>ment, accid<u>e</u>nt, aer<u>o</u>plane, ambul<u>a</u>nce, bus driv<u>er</u>, childr<u>e</u>n, cigarette, cin<u>e</u>ma, doct<u>or</u>, ladd<u>er</u>, letterbox, mot<u>or</u>bike, newsagent's, newspap<u>er</u>, pass<u>e</u>ngers, pavem<u>e</u>nt, p<u>e</u>destrian, petr<u>o</u>l stati<u>o</u>n, ph<u>o</u>togra<u>ph</u>er, p<u>o</u>licem<u>a</u>n, stretch<u>er</u>, s<u>u</u>permarket, window clean<u>er</u>, wom<u>a</u>n.

Ways of spelling the sound /ə/ include: *or*, *e*, *a*, *o* and *er*.

Unit 64 Pronouncing single vowel letters

2
U.S.A.	=	The United States of America
E.C.	=	The European Community
P.T.O.	=	Please Turn Over
I.O.U.	=	I Owe You
U.N.	=	The United Nations
U.K.	=	The United Kingdom
U.A.E.	=	The United Arab Emirates
W.H.O.	=	The World Health Organisation

4
c<u>a</u>ke	fact	g<u>a</u>me	l<u>i</u>fe	tap	cup	test	h<u>o</u>me	th<u>e</u>se
left	bit	t<u>u</u>ne	spell	bag	drop	pl<u>a</u>ne	m<u>i</u>ne	t<u>u</u>be
soft	n<u>o</u>se	kill	dust

6 When a one-syllable word ends with C+e (i.e. a single consonant followed by the letter 'e'), the vowel letter is pronounced with its name.

Unit 65 Pronouncing vowel pairs

2 Most likely answers:

1 three	5 between	9 eighteen	13 school
2 spoon	6 cheap	10 sleep	14 eat
3 wool	7 afternoon	11 easy	15 already
4 clean	8 cooking	12 heavy	16 break

3 Possible answers:

	/iː/	/uː/	/e/	/ʊ/	/eɪ/
'ee'	three, between, eighteen, sleep (4)	✗	✗	✗	✗
'oo'	✗	spoon, afternoon, school (3)	✗	wool, cooking (2)	✗
'ea'	clean, cheap, easy, eat (4)	✗	heavy, already (2)	✗	break (1)

4 A: How was the holiday?
B: <u>Marvellous</u>.
A: Switzerland, wasn't it?
B: That's right. It's a beautiful <u>country</u>.
A: Did a <u>group</u> of <u>you</u> go?
B: No, just me and my <u>cousin</u>.
A: Where did you stay?
B: We rented a <u>house</u> in Zurich.
A: How was the weather?
B: Well, a bit <u>cloudy</u>.
A: Lots of shopping?
B: Oh, yes. Lots of <u>souvenirs</u>. And I <u>found</u> this <u>blouse</u>.
A: Lovely. Did you go skiing, too?
B: Yes, we went <u>south</u> to the <u>mountains</u>.
A: I've never been skiing. It <u>sounds</u> too <u>dangerous</u>.
B: Well, I had a few falls, but nothing too <u>serious</u>.
A: And will you go back?
B: Probably. The only <u>trouble</u> was, there were too many <u>tourists</u>!
But you've been on holiday, too, haven't you? How was <u>yours</u>?
A: Oh, we had a really good time …

6 1 marvellous, dangerous, serious   /ə/
2 country, cousin, trouble   /ʊ/
3 group, you, souvenirs   /uː/
4 house, cloudy, found, blouse, south, mountains, sounds   /aʊ/
5 tourists, yours   /ɔː/

Unit 66 Silent letters

1 cupboard   climb   knee   island   half   autumn   know   handkerchief   listen   knife   hour   two   Christmas   answer   comb   honest   talk   handsome

3 interesting   police   chocolate   secretary   factory   several   average   postman   different   family   government   medicine   strawberries   aspirin   dustbin   favourite

5

How often do you play football?	Twice a week on average.
Would you like some sweets?	I've already had some chocolate.
What's on the news?	The government's resigned.
We've been robbed!	Call the police.
Who did you go on holiday with?	I went with my family.
What shall we have for pudding?	Strawberries and ice cream.
What's in the bottle?	Some medicine for my cold.
What do you think of this cheese?	It's my favourite.
Are these packets the same?	No, they're different.
Have you ever been to Paris?	Several times.